EYES ON
THE MODERN WORLD

EYES ON
THE MODERN WORLD

Views on Schema 13

Edited by JOHN G. DEEDY, Jr.

RICHARD HORCHLER   SIDNEY CORNELIA CALLAHAN
MICHAEL NOVAK   ADOLPH SCHALK
DONALD QUINN   JAMES DOUGLASS
JOHN G. DEEDY, Jr.   CLAUD NELSON

P. J. Kenedy & Sons   :   *New York*

Contents

About the Authors

RICHARD HORCHLER is national program director of the National Conference of Christians and Jews, an organization of religiously motivated individuals who seek to relate their religious beliefs to the problems of public life in America. From 1957 to 1962 Mr. Horchler was an associate editor of *The Commonweal*, national weekly edited and published by Catholic laymen. Before that he was an assistant professor of English at St. Peter's College, New Jersey, and Fordham University, New York. He was educated at Regis High School, N. Y., Columbia College, and Columbia University. He has lectured on religious, Church-State, and civic questions, and written for *The Commonweal, Jubilee, Ave Maria, Worldview, The Lamp*, Religious News Service, *The Christian Century*, the *New York Times Book Review* and other publications.

MICHAEL NOVAK is the author of *The Open Church* (Macmillan), *A New Generation* (Herder and Herder), and of a novel *The Tiber Was Silver* (Doubleday). He edited the book, *The Experience of Marriage* (Macmillan), and has published in *Concilium, Theological Studies*, the *Journal of Ecumenical Studies*, etc. He has studied theology at the Gregorian University, and the history and philosophy of religion at Harvard, and is now an assistant professor of Religion at Stanford.

DONALD QUINN is the editorial section editor of the *St. Louis Review*, one of the country's leading Catholic newspapers. For

7

eighteen years he has been a newspaper reporter, writer, and editor, concentrating in the fields of politics, social welfare, and economics. He was a reporter for a small Texas daily and the Associated Press before he moved into desk positions at the *Lincoln* (Neb.) *Star* and *The Washington Post*, where he was assistant city editor. In 1960 he became the founding managing editor of a new diocesan weekly, *The Oklahoma Courier*, which quickly was recognized as one of the most aggressive U.S. Catholic newspapers. He joined the *St. Louis Review* in 1963 and has covered social problems and Vatican Council II as a reporter for his newspaper. Mr. Quinn has fulfilled writing assignments for the Catholic Features Cooperative, *Sign*, *Ave Maria*, *Marriage*, *The Commonweal*, *The Living Light*, and other publications. He is a contributor to the volumes *Masterpieces of Catholic Literature*.

JOHN G. DEEDY, JR. has been associated with the Catholic press since 1951. He was the founding editor of *The Catholic Free Press* of Worcester, Mass., and since 1959 has been editor of the *Pittsburgh Catholic*. Previously he was associated with the daily press. His work has appeared in *The Commonweal*, *America*, *The Critic*, *Ave Maria*, *U.S. Catholic* and *The Sign*. He is co-author of the book *The Religious Press in America* (Holt, Rinehart and Winston); contributor to *Federal Aid and Catholic Schools* (Helicon), and editor of *The Church in Worcester, New England* (Hawthorne).

SIDNEY CORNELIA CALLAHAN, a *magna cum laude* graduate of Bryn Mawr College, has written for *Ave Maria*, *The Critic* and *The Catholic World*. She is the author of *The Illusion of Eve: Modern Woman's Quest for Identity* (Sheed & Ward), and contributor to the book *What Modern Catholics Think About Birth Control* (Signet). She is the mother of six children and the wife of Daniel Callahan, an associate editor of *The Commonweal*.

ADOLPH SCHALK is a free-lance American writer who has been living in Europe for the past ten years and presently makes his headquarters near Zurich, Switzerland. His journalistic experience includes a brief period as an editorial assistant to the late Reverend Daniel A. Lord, S.J., at The Queen's Work, Publishers, St. Louis; as former editor of *Today;* and as founding editor of *The Bridge,* a monthly newspaper published by Atlantik-Brucke (Atlantic Bridge), a nonpartisan West German association devoted to furthering German-American understanding. He has worked as correspondent for Religious News Service and has carried out special assignments for *Time*, *Life*, NCWC News Service, and for Harry Golden, editor of *The Carolina Israelite*. His work has appeared in *U.S. Catholic*, *The Commonweal*, *The Sign*, *The National Catholic Reporter*, *Stars and Stripes*, *Pittsburgh Catholic*, *The Sydney Morning Herald*, *America*, *Jubilee*, and *Catholic Digest*. In 1964 Mr. Schalk won first prize from the Catholic Press Association for the best nonfiction article, "Behind the Wall," describing living conditions in East Berlin. The article appeared in the April, 1963, issue of *The Sign*.

JAMES DOUGLASS was graduated from the University of Santa Clara in 1960 and studied English in the Graduate School of the University of Kansas. He received an M.A. in theology from the University of Notre Dame in 1962 and then spent two years in Rome with his family where he studied theology at the Gregorian University. He has written for *Cross Currents*, *Perspectives*, *Downside Review*, *The Commonweal*, *The Catholic Worker*, *Worldview*, *Ave Maria*, and *The Catholic World*. He is now an assistant professor of theology at Bellarmine College in Louisville, Kentucky.

REVEREND CLAUD D. NELSON, M.A., Oxon., Hon. LL.D., Hendrix College, and Rhodes scholar from Arkansas, 1910-13, is a fifth generation Methodist minister. He has spent fifty-one years in the ministry of "the Church in the World" (sixteen in Europe): teaching, Y.M.C.A., Fellowship of Reconciliation, National Council of Churches, National Conference of Christians and Jews. He engaged in relief work during and after World Wars I and II for prisoners of war and students, and has been active in race relations, international and ecumenical affairs. He is editor of *The Dialogue Bulletin*, and has been a special correspondent in Rome for Religious News Service, covering Vatican Council preparations and the three sessions to date. He expects to attend the fourth session. Dr. Nelson is author of *The Vatican Council and All Christians* (Association Press).

For Four Blessings . . .
Joan, John, Justine and Paul . . .
May their Modern World be blessed

Editor's Foreword

In the ideal order of things, nothing should provide greater insurance against Vatican Council II settling into history as an esoteric experience—theologically, liturgically, ecumenically, whatever—than Schema 13, "The Church in the Modern World." This is not to say that the success of Vatican II depends exclusively on the fate of Schema 13, but it is to suggest that the total success of the Council will not be unrelated to the final disposition of the Council with regard to Schema 13.

For Schema 13 is the document which brings the Church in confrontation with the issues which are the everyday concern not only of her institutional self, not only of those she is pleased to call "the People of God," but of the entire human family. It is in its own way the "bread-and-butter" schema of Vatican Council II—the document that speaks to man on the level of his hopes and anxieties, his problems and his aspirations, his living and his breathing. It is the schema that deals with mundane matters, but urgencies foremost in man's mind: such as war and peace, family planning, poverty, leisure time, economic security, community action.

The schema on the Church in the modern world was of be-
lated thought and nervous fulfillment. It is the creature, almost
in the literal sense, of Leo Joseph Cardinal Suenens, Archbishop of Malines-Brussels. He it was who, in the final days of
Session One, when Council Fathers were debating *De Ecclesia*,
the schema on the nature of the Church, proposed a document
which would add dimension to the dialogue the Church was
having with and of itself by establishing a dialogue with and
of the modern world. The date was December 4, 1962; Vatican Council II was in its 33rd General Congregation.

Two years (October 20, 1964) and seventy-two Council
meetings later (the 105th General Congregation), the schema
on the Church in the modern world came officially before the
Fathers, its outline corresponding remarkably to the one
sketched by Cardinal Suenens that December day in 1962. In
behalf of the mixed Theological Commission and Commission
for the Lay Apostolate which drew up the working draft,
Fernando Cardinal Cento of the Roman Curia commented that
"it is more than clear that, especially today, the Church cannot
remain closed up within herself as in a fortress, intent only on
defending her own interests and members." Hence, he explained, the Council "passes to a discussion of the burning
problems tormenting today."

The document introduced at last to the Fathers contained
an introduction, four chapters and a conclusion, and covered
some twenty-five pages of legal-sized stationery. Although the
schema, by its own admission, did not offer answers to all the
political, social, and economic problems of the times, it did aim
to define the issues and offer guidelines, and it did prod men
"to enter upon the most urgent tasks of our day with a valiant
spirit and vigorous zeal." This was a new and exciting approach for an institution not always noted for intellectual
humility and for anxiousness to encourage individual initiative.

The draft presented to the Council Fathers carried the following chapter titles: "Man's Complete Vocation," "The
Church Dedicated to the Service of God and Man," "The

Conduct of Christians in the World in Which They Live," and "The Chief Duties to Be Fulfilled by Christians of Our Day." The schema dealt primarily with attitudes and principles. Specifics and practicalities were grouped into five appendices. The appendices were not submitted to the Fathers for debate, merely as auxiliary instruments in the study of the conciliar text.

Theoretically the Fathers were to confine their interventions to the principles of the schema, but from the moment debate opened there seemed little timidity about coming to grips with specifics. The high point in directness arrived when Cardinal Suenens, Bernard Cardinal Alfrink of Utrecht, Emile Cardinal Léger of Montreal and the Melchite Patriarch (now Cardinal), Maximos IV Saigh of Antioch, spoke bluntly and without being interrupted on the theology of marriage.

This book is not necessarily a parallel venture in bluntness, but it is an attempt to discuss directly some of the specifics to which the principles of the schema apply. The book focuses on several of the thought units of the schema and examines these in the light of the logic of the schema and the essayists' concepts of what the posture of the Church, her members, and humanity generally should or might be in given areas of interest. The essayists use as a starting point the draft of the schema which was presented to the Fathers during Session Three. It is realized, of course, that this draft is undergoing extensive revision; yet the draft is still useful for the broad indications it gives of the relationships which the Church considers to be hers to the temporal world. Where relevant to their subject matter, the essayists take into account Session Three interventions on Schema 13.

This volume is intended less to "counsel the Council" than to present the opinions and the hopes of representative members of the laity. Much of what the writers say may be provocative; much may be controversial; much may even prove disharmonious with certain sections of the schema finally voted by the Fathers. But all is advanced in a spirit of love for the One True God and concern for the world that is His.

The inspiration for the book arises in part from the fact that Schema 13 is addressed to "the Church's children"—"in the hope," as the schema words it, "that with their combined efforts they will do their part in building a world according to the spirit of Christ." Since "the Church's children" are being addressed, it seems reasonable that they should also be heard.

The inspiration springs secondarily from the mandate contained in the constitution on the nature of the Church, promulgated by Pope Paul VI at the conclusion of Session Three: "They [the laity] should openly reveal to them [their pastors] their needs and desires with that freedom and confidence which is fitting for children of God and brothers in Christ. They are, by reason of the knowledge, competence, or outstanding ability which they may enjoy, permitted and sometimes even obliged to express their opinion on those things which concern the good of the Church." The contributors to this book consider Schema 13 a concern obliging the expression of opinion.

With the exception of Mrs. Sidney Callahan, who has special qualifications to commend her inclusion in this symposium, the essayists for the book were all present in Rome during the fall of 1964, as the gestation period for Schema 13 reached the terminal point. They therefore bring to their essays an interest and intimacy heightened by firsthand observation and study.

A non-Catholic, one who has been in Rome for all Council sessions to date, joins in the symposium, adding a perspective for which the Church voices anxiety in the schema. Section 3 of the prologue spells out the desire that the schema will be heard by "the beloved brethren of the communities of the Church that are separated from us."

We perhaps should also have included a Jew, since the schema speaks the hope of reaching with its message those "who have not yet come to acknowledge Christ" but who "give thanks with us to the living and holy God"; we might also have included an agnostic, or even an atheist, since the schema likewise aims at those of no belief at all. However, it is because the schema stresses "cooperation . . . especially with our separated brethren," and because concern for the schema appears most immediate with Protestants, that one of their number writes with us. His essay ranges over the whole of the schema, while the others are limited to given topics.

The aspiration of all the essayists is modest: to make some small contribution to building what Schema 13 terms "a truly fraternal earthly city." May it be so.

JOHN G. DEEDY, JR.

Pittsburgh, 1965

I

The Church's 'Yes' and 'No' to the World

by RICHARD HORCHLER

IF the *aggiornamento* is to succeed, then of course the Roman
Catholic Church must come to terms with the modern world.
That is what *aggiornamento* means and what Pope John's
vision was principally about. But coming to terms with the
modern world will involve not merely a little retooling of the
machinery here and there, improving the efficiency of this or
that ecclesial process, but the most radical, revolutionary
change in the Church's fundamental conception of herself and
her mission. In other words, the Church has problems in its
relation to the modern world not only because it has failed to
keep step in a rapidly changing modern world, but because it
has had grievous problems always in its relation to the world;
that is, to the temporal, secular order itself, apart from the
special problems of any particular historical period.

The relation of Christianity to any given culture—to the

fabric of civilization in a particular time and place, including the mind-set, concepts, and values of that civilization as well as its arts, sciences, and institutions—is another problem, but one immediately linked to the larger question of the Christian's over-all attitude toward the world and the flesh. And if Christianity has been for most of its life less anxious about its relation to culture than about its relation to the world itself, we have come to realize now that it *should* have been more anxious about this relation to culture.

Unconscious and uncritical culture-identification has brought Christianity as a whole to its status today as pre-eminently the religion of the white man or of the West. It has brought Roman Catholicism to its present struggle to escape from the bonds of *Romanità* and American Protestantism to its recent traumatic discovery that it is not synonymous with the American Way of Life. Since culture-identification in the form of medievalism has contributed largely to the inability of the Catholic Church to relate to the modern world, and since the modern world is the only world that now exists, culture-identification has also crippled the development of a true Catholic theology of the world.

It is cause for great joy that in the Council the Church has been facing up to the problem of its role in the affairs of men on earth and the problem of its relation to particular cultures. The constitutions on the Church and the Liturgy already reflect profoundly important advances in Roman Catholic understanding of what the Church is, how it must work in the world and must adapt itself to the languages and habits of different peoples in the family of man. It is encouraging, too, that the Council Fathers have been grappling with a statement specifically on the Church in the modern world, Schema 13.

About the schema itself, however—that is, the draft accepted for discussion in the Council's Third Session and being amended as I write—it is possible to have, at best, only mixed feelings. Perhaps the first thing to say about it is that, in translation and, I am assured, in Latin, it shows that the Church does not speak in the accents of the modern world actually as well as figuratively. What the schema says is for the most part, and especially between the lines, a reassuring statement of the *aggiornamento*-type sentiments that used to be liberal heresies. But it is disappointing that the Council Fathers did not give the schema the time and preparation it deserves. For instance, the crucial section of the draft on culture, article 22, was called "almost the nucleus of our entire schema" by Giacomo Cardinal Lercaro of Bologna. Yet this section, which I would call "almost the nucleus of the entire *aggiornamento*," consists of only six paragraphs.

Furthermore, I wonder what meaning the schema's affirmations can possibly have to those it addresses until its avowals are pulled out of the historical vacuum of the draft and fixed in a context. The schema seems to be offering answers, but answers cannot be appreciated in the absence of the questions. For this Catholic, formulation of the proper questions about the Church in culture and in the world requires a look at the whole experience of the Church in the world. And while it may be true that an overview is an oversimplification, it is true also that complexities, to be grasped, must be reduced and sorted out in simpler terms.

The root problem is, in my understanding of Christian history, that Christianity has from the beginning been plagued by ambiguity, if not confusion, in its participation in particular cultures and, more fundamentally, in its entire attitude toward this world. Primitive Christians, as we know, turned their backs on the world. Convinced that time was rushing to an end, that the Second Coming was imminent, they took no interest in the outcome of worldly affairs. The business of the Christian, who felt himself to be not only a temporary resident but actually an alien in the world, was to keep himself uncontaminated and ready for the Kingdom. Hence the separation and asceticism of the early Christian communities, the exaltation of virginity and the disparagement of marriage except as a refuge from sin, the rejection of all things merely human as snares and delusions to the pilgrim who was in but not of the world.

As for the earliest Christian's relation to his culture, it seems to have been, understandably, unconscious at first, with no suspicion that the Jewish way of thinking, Jewish habits of life, Jewish heritage of ritual and worship were not "natural" and "essential" to the religion which was then Jewish-Christianity. But very soon, as a result of the evangelization of other peoples, the Church was faced with its first culture-crisis. The resolution of that crisis, at the meeting described in the Acts of the Apostles and thought of now as the first Council of the Church, determined forever that Christianity was a universal faith, not to be conscribed by any one culture.

Afterward, however, the process of culture-identification began to work again. The Church historians tell us that when Paul and Barnabas were upheld in their dispensation of Gentile converts from the Judaic Law, for a time the Church was in its life bicultural or multicultural. Before many more centuries had passed, however, the Church we know in the West was once again embodied essentially in one culture, this time the Greco-Roman. This came about as a result of many things: Jewish-Christian hostility over Christian rejection of the precepts of the Old Law, which led to further de-Judaization; the destruction of the Temple at Jerusalem and the dispersion of the Jews there; Roman persecution of the Jews in Palestine; the success of Paul and others in their missions to the Gentiles; the congeniality of Greek philosophy and ways of thinking to the message of the Gospel; the synthesizing power of Hellenistic thought and Roman law.

At any rate, as a result of these and other pressures, joined with the explosive force of the Good News of salvation, the center of gravity in the early Christian Church moved westward. The Edict of Milan, in A.D. 313, ended the persecutions of the Christians and proclaimed Rome's admission that the new religion could not be stamped out by terror, torture, and martyrdom. By A.D. 380, Christianity was the State religion of the Roman Empire, and with the Empire went further westward.

In this new position of privilege, power, and temporal responsibility, despite vicissitudes and reverses in the centuries that followed, the Westernization or Romanization of at least one branch of the Church was both symbolized and intensified. Its Greco-Roman character was to be seen not only in language, ritual, art, and music, not only in form, organization and emphasis on law, but in its habit of mind and mode of thought, its inevitable conception of itself in terms of its past experience. So the Church in the West assumed the Greek bent toward speculation and dualism, the Roman habits of discipline, system, and authority.

The Jewish cultural element had been lost, or repudiated, by Christianity early. Subsequently, the Church in the East and the Church in the West were gradually alienated from each other because of the increasingly hopeless tangle of doctrinal, jurisdictional, and political disputes which culminated in the eleventh century Great Schism. The division had been exacerbated, if not provoked, by wholly nonreligious conflicts —East-West rivalry in language, culture, political, and economic power—and by the identification of Church and State in both East and West. By the time of the Crusades, the Latin and Eastern Churches were not only separated but thoroughly identified with mutually hostile, rival cultures.

To the Roman Church, which had of course maintained its dedication to the primacy of Peter and had anathematized the heresies, schisms, and ecclesiastical vendettas that plagued the Eastern sees, a natural conclusion emerged. The one, true Church was Latin, and the only structures, traditions, doctrinal emphases and even culture that had been able to keep the bark of Peter safe and steady through the storms were those of the Church of Rome. This meant something like divine approbation for the order of things in a medieval, Latin European, Church-dominated society, as well as in the medieval,

Latin European Church. Church and society in fact had become coterminous.

In these centuries the Schoolmen, and pre-eminently St. Thomas, were able to do for the Roman Church in philosophy and theology what imperial Rome had done for it in language, organization, and administration. St. Thomas provided an all-inclusive, seemingly perfect and immutable system of thought, accommodating and integrating to a fantastic degree every category of knowledge in his world. St. Thomas's system, which has become *the* philosophy of the Roman Catholic Church, was also, of course, firmly Western and medieval.

So was accomplished the almost total identification of the one, holy, apostolic and *Catholic* Church with a particular civilization, with the language, arts, institutions, patterns of public and private life, philosophy, and theology of medieval, Latin Europe. In justice, it must be noted that such an identification of culture and religion looks much more disastrous and grotesque to those who are outside the culture in question —outside it in time, space, or acceptance. The Latin medievals lacked the advantages of cultural anthropology and comparative religion, the experience of diversity and pluralism which characterizes the modern world. It was possible for them to think of Christendom as encompassing at least the "civilized" world, wherein the Latin language, Latin learning, and the Church were indeed "universal."

Furthermore, as a river takes its color from the bed over which it flows, it is altogether natural for religion to assume coloration from the culture in which it has its life, even the universal, supracultural religion which is Christianity. The disaster occurs when the supposedly universal religion is held to be identical with the culture in which it works—or when some mighty phenomenon brings a shift in the river bed and changes the course of the river. Then those who have identified the river with the bed are left with no more than a trickle, or even a dried-out channel, while the living water rushes elsewhere.

But what had the experiences of a dozen or so centuries meant in the attitudes of the Church toward the world, toward temporal existence? The early Church had been "world-fleeing." Christ had said, explicitly enough, "My kingdom is not of this world," and His followers chose to live only in and for that otherworldly kingdom. They felt little interest in or responsibility for the blind and foolish enterprises of those who lived in darkness. Loving one another, they gathered in communities of the elect and waited for the apocalyptic fulfillment and their deliverance from the world, the flesh and the devil—which they believed would come soon.

Since the deliverance did not come soon, the Christians were constrained to reply to the demands that were made of them as human beings in the world, with bodies (however "vile") as well as souls. Still, the adjustment they made to the world was for the most part reluctant, minimal, and to be justified only by pressing material or spiritual necessity. Even the end of the Roman persecutions under Constantine, and the establishment of Christianity as the State religion of the Roman Empire did not mean that Christians ceased to "despise the world," at least as they conceived the Christian ideal.

What the assumption of secular power did mean for the early Church, apparently, was the beginning of ambivalence and self-contradiction in the approach to the things of this world. Abnegation of the flesh and disdain for the vanities of this life were as central as ever in Christian thought, but the new situation of the Church brought a pragmatic acceptance of the responsibilities and opportunities it presented. Over the centuries, as the institutional Church became more and more entangled with the authority of the State, as it became stronger, wealthier, more and more involved with temporal power, the more schizophrenic the medieval Christian view appears from our vantage point today. On the one hand, those revered as its greatest saints were the martyrs, virgins, anchorites, mystics; on the other hand, the Church itself claimed all power and all authority in the world, challenged kings

and emperors for temporal might, surrounded its pope and h
court with pomp and splendor.

There are many explanations and extenuations for such
paradox, I know, not least that of human frailty in the face
temptation. But there may be more illumination in not soft
ing the paradox in medieval Christian attitudes toward __
world, for from it emerges the firm conclusion that the medieval Church, despite its dozen or more centuries of involvement in human affairs, had never come fully to accept the
temporal as worthy of or entitled to religious respect. The
Church's tendency was either "world-fleeing" or—if the
chance were presented—"world-coercing," seldom anything
in between. Then, as always, there were the vital currents in
Christianity which carried the idea of worth and dignity in all
of God's creation, but more often than not these affirmations
were forgotten.

In broad outline, the high middle ages brought a Catholic
Church whose characteristic official posture toward the world
was, at best, ambiguous. It preached renunciation of the world
and the flesh, but as it found itself in this life able to appropriate power, it seized this power and exploited it to advance its
own interests, which included the glorification of God through
the earthly glorification of His Church. Such a contradiction
was encouraged by the idea that since the Christian's true
morality lay in transcending the flesh, actual worldly affairs
were therefore outside morality altogether. Thus the failure of
the Church to develop teachings on the Christian's and the
Church's responsibility in the real, fallen world of, for instance, politics, social human relations, sex, and marriage. Side
by side with characteristic medieval piety, then—and to a significant degree because of the nature of that piety—flourished
equally characteristic medieval cruelty, sensual indulgence,
and cynicism. These centuries gave us great saints, the monas-
tic movement, and also such anomalies as holy wars, the terri-
torial entity of "Christendom," and the Holy Roman Empire.

Summing up the developing attitudes of the Church toward

culture and toward the temporal, at this point in history the Roman Church identified itself thoroughly and unquestioningly with the culture of Latin Europe. As for the world, for the most part the Church treated it as fallen and sinful, not to be perfected but transcended; at the same time, where the Church had power it did not hesitate to order the world, through force if necessary, in a way more pleasing to itself. And since it was "not of this world," the Church in its teachings tended to save men by taking them *out* of the world, to the monastery or its mental and emotional equivalent, rather than to save them *in* the world. To the culture in which it dwelled, the Church said a contented *Yes*. To the temporal world it said an apparently contradictory, sometimes hypocritical, often anguished *Yes* and *No*. And it was then that Catholic Europe began to disintegrate.

Some day the story of the Church in the past four or five centuries—and possibly in the next century or more—may be compressed into a single chapter with a title something like "Metamorphosis." For what is involved here, at least in my conception of it, is an uncompleted unity: the ending of one stage in human history, one stage in the life of Christianity, and the development of the next.

The elements in this agony are enormous: the end of medievalism, the destruction of Catholic—even Christian—Europe, the death struggles of the absolute kings, the Protestant Reformation, the Counter Reformation, the French Revolution, Enlightenment, anticlericalism, secularism. The lines of thought and action are tangled by contradictions, reverses, and obscurities, symbolized by this period's bewildering succession of dissonant leaders: popes and kings, philosophers and polemicists, reformers, rebels, reactionaries, and visionaries.

Adequate treatment of these subjects is in the first place beyond the scope of this paper and the capabilities of its author, but in the second place unnecessary to the limited purposes of this enterprise. What can be done here is to set down an understanding, not of the individual events, documents, teachings of these times, but of what all these sift down to in terms of one great phenomenon and its effect, ultimately, on the Roman Catholic Church.

Obviously, the Protestant Reformation had profoundly important consequences in Catholicism's stance toward both culture and the world, as well as in everything else in its life. Catholics can admit today, in this ecumenical age, that the Church in the time of Luther was in need of reform and that the early reformers, if many things had been different, could have remained only reformers. The tragedy is that the Church then did not, or could not, go into dialogue with itself. Instead, the parties in the disputes were isolated from each other, and the contending ideas were not just frozen but exaggerated on both sides. For instance, insofar as Lutheran and other reforming doctrines tended to denigrate asceticism, monasticism, juridicism, and discipline, the Roman reaction was to strengthen its commitment to these ideas. Insofar as Protestantism allied itself with the forces that were destroying the old, medieval Catholic world—the rise of nationalism, capitalism, individualism, libertarianism—Protestantism and the new order were linked together and denounced as one. And insofar as Protestantism was identified with the Germans, English, Scandinavians, et al., so the Roman Church tended all the more to turn in upon its Latinism.

The other great force of these tumultuous centuries, of course, was the secular thrust toward the overthrow of the entire *ancien régime*. This meant revolution in political structure, social order, in traditional learning—and in the role of religion. The major prophets of this movement were hostile to the temporal claims of the Church, its political power, cultural influence, its doctrines and even its right to exist. They were also, in the Europe of this time, the only strong advocates of freedom, human equality, social justice, and progress. But they were revolutionaries; as a threatened temporal power, the Church was their natural enemy, and an enemy to their ideas of republicanism and democracy. Furthermore, the allies of the Church in these bloody years were the absolutists and royalists who were also threatened by the revolutionary tide, like the Bourbons whose name today has become the accepted term for blind reaction.

By the nineteenth century the destruction of the old world was complete, and in the process of its destruction the Church of Rome had suffered shocks that are today almost incalculable. When the first tremors of the cataclysm were felt, the Church was presiding over a world that was its own. It claimed jurisdiction over all mankind, commanded kings and emperors, breathed in a culture it had in large measure built and shaped in accordance with its teachings. Now the Church was hardly more than a survivor. In a few centuries' time, it had been, on almost every side, defied, torn, ravaged, beaten, and repudiated. Millions of its followers had defected; bishops, priests, monasteries, convents, whole nations had been lost, with cathedrals, abbeys, the ancient universities, treasures beyond price. Except for a beleaguered little corner of Rome, the temporal sovereignty of the Church had been not only challenged but defeated and destroyed. Christendom had vanished, and in its place was an alien world of strange, new, secularized States.

Most shocking of all, perhaps, was the blow to the Church's sense of mission as the divinely appointed teacher to the world. Worse, no doubt, than the defiance the Church had known in the past was the mere contempt it had earned in the eyes of the modern world. The great weapon of the French *philosophes* had been laughter and mockery. And now, in the forming modern, secular culture, the Catholic Church was less a serious adversary than simply an irrelevancy, a fossil.

Nevertheless, the Roman Catholic Church did manage to survive. That it has done so, and continues to be regenerated after countless apparent deaths, is to the believer proof of its establishment by God and the abiding presence in it of the

Holy Spirit. To the unbeliever its survival must be at least an amazement.

The response the Church made to the assaults of these centuries included authority, anathemas, diplomacy and armed might—to no avail—but also the Counter Reformation. Stretching over more than a hundred years, this process aimed at no reconciliation with the theological and human ideas of the Reformation, but rather a mobilization of Catholic strength in resisting these ideas. One of its results was a hardening of the doctrines and characteristics which had been challenged by the Reformation; for instance, traditionalism, objectivism, sacramentalism, scholasticism. Another result, however, was an almost miraculous success in rooting out what were probably the more important causes of the Reformation: ignorance, faithlessness, corruption and vice in the clergy, bishops, and even papacy. Symbolized by the Council of Trent, in 1545, and continued under several reforming popes—the most notable of whom, incidentally, was named Paul—the Counter Reformation accomplished educational and administrative overhaul, the cleansing of the papacy and hierarchy from avarice and licentiousness, the imposition of rigorous discipline, the restoration of the religious orders, the recovery of the sense of spiritual identity and purpose.

In its attitude toward the culture in which it found itself, however, the Catholic Church made a complete reversal. Since it saw the post-Reformation and post-French Revolution culture, with a few exceptions, as heretical, impious, anarchic, and depraved, its response to it was violent rejection. The values which animated modern Western culture—science, material advancement, freedom, equality—the Church of Rome dismissed as merely pretty words for the evils of irreligion, sensuality, license, and relativism. There could be no identification of Catholicism with this modern way of life.

In this situation there was, moreover, little possibility of change. The Church had always had to adjust to new conditions in an evolving culture, but it made its adjustment as a recognized, integral part of the social structure. Now the Church was denied its traditional role in the society, and it was unable or as yet unwilling to develop an entirely new role. Its desire was to try to bring back the culture in which it had known security, power, even dominance—the culture it thought of as its *own* culture, that of the Catholic middle ages. Of course this effort failed, and the next best thing was for Catholics to maintain a private medieval culture within the modern culture in which they lived. Hence Roman Catholic nostalgia for the good old days and the "thirteenth, greatest of centuries." Catholicism's uncritical, enthusiastic *Yes* to the culture of the times had become an uncompromising, all-inclusive *No*, typified in Pius IX's broadside "Syllabus of Errors" in 1864.

Catholic attitudes toward the world and worldly things were also bound to be affected by the estrangement between religion, and Catholicism particularly, and the increasingly secularized modern culture. One result of this alienation, no doubt reinforced by reaction to Protestant stress on the Christian's social role, was an even greater emphasis on otherworldliness, interior life and sexual denial—in Catholic preachment if not practice. In ages past, the major alternative to flight from the world for the Church had been coercion of the world, the assumption of authority over the City of Man. But this kind of response was now impossible, except to a degree in certain Latin countries and sporadically or indirectly in those others where Catholics were numerous. A third alternative—acceptance, witness and loving service, even in a hostile or indifferent environment—required a conception of itself, the world and culture which the Church had never formed, partly because it had never been forced to.

It might appear, then, that Roman Catholicism had reached a point where, theoretically, and according to its old patterns, it had no way to relate to the social world. But such an idea, even if it could be believed, could not revoke the fact that Catholics were flesh and blood creatures, social beings, who ate, worked, voted, painted pictures, loved their wives, their

neighbors, and their country—and tried to do all those things
without ceasing to be Catholics. Nonparticipation in the culture in which one lives is a practical impossibility. And as they
lived in this anathematized, often Protestantized, secularized
modern culture, most strikingly where it was truly pluralistic
and truly free, increasing numbers of Catholics—priests, bishops and theologians, as well as laymen—found it to be good.
In the new order, religious liberty, separation of Church and
State, democracy and other "errors" seemed, in practice, and
most self-evidently to American Catholics, to be best for the
common welfare and best for religion.

As for Catholic concern for the temporal, natural impulses
and growing involvement with neighbors in many cases combined easily with the often forgotten but never wholly lost
Christian precepts of fraternal love and social responsibility
inherent in Catholicism, strengthened perhaps by secular hu-
manitarianism and contact with socially energetic Protestantism. The result was that many zealous Catholics found themselves laboring alongside their "heretical" and "atheist" brothers for human betterment in the here-and-now and similar
"Social Gospel" causes. Moreover, as the nineteenth century
wore into the twentieth, the Church through hierarchy and
even pope spoke favorably, now and again, and here and there
in the world, on certain values and ideas which it had once
branded impious. Official Church agencies and institutions
sometimes pursued goals and used methods in political, economic, social, educational, and cultural enterprises that had
once been deplored, if not denounced, by Rome. Periodically,
high-ranking prelates and other Catholic spokesmen publicly
urged abandonment of the mid-nineteenth century condemna-
tions and called for a kind of *aggiornamento*, although the
term had not yet been thought of. The high point of this
liberalizing movement, which encouraged social reform, political engagement and responsibility in the temporal order,
probably came in late nineteenth century America under the
inspiration of Father Isaac Hecker, James Cardinal Gibbons,

Church "will gladly renounce the exercise of certain legitimately acquired rights" in the civil order, if the use of such rights calls into doubt the "sincerity of her witness." Also in this section—again, in the original—is an affirmation of belief in religious liberty for everyone, which can hardly be more unequivocal, although I have not seen it, in the much heralded and long delayed Declaration on Religious Liberty. The section goes on to say, almost offhandedly, that the spiritual and temporal authorities "must be kept distinct." Most notable of all, perhaps, in these general passages, is the counsel to the faithful not to "think that their pastors are either competent or called to give them an answer to all questions, even the serious ones" that confront the Christian in the world. This last is heady stuff in the proverbial Roman Catholic "monolith."

The weaknesses and flaws in the entire document are large—and more will be said of them—but similarly "liberal" or "modern" or "Social Gospel" ideas are more or less characteristic of its approach. Following the style of the "new" Catholic Church, it concludes with words to those "who do not yet love the Church, or are even opposed to her, and sometimes even persecute her . . . not only to forgive them, but also to ask their pardon, if the defects of Christians have been a scandal to them."

What is best in the schema is its tone, which is positive and generous. The more general introductory sections, particularly, present teachings—or preachings—about the Christian role of witness and service in the world that Catholics have not much heard and that will do much good, if they are heeded. The sections on particular aspects of the Christian's social concern, however, are uneven, fragmentary and in the main unsatisfying. Article 22, on the pivotal question of religious-cultural interaction, may well be the poorest effort in this group, although other critics will have their own selections for this honor.

Like everything else in the schema, the paragraphs on culture reflect the right—to me—sentiments in general. The schema does say clearly that the Church is "not bound exclusively to any particular culture, but . . . enters into communion with all cultures." Insofar as I can penetrate the murkiness of the text, the arts and sciences seem to be commended as good things. And, again presuming I have correctly translated the translation, there may even be here an approval of the kind of serious or modern art, frequently deplored by Catholics, in the approbation of works in which "the profound problems of human life are presented more clearly," as well as those that appeal to the "sense of the beautiful."

Much of the treatment of culture is routine, vague and tangled in several overlapping uses of the word *culture*. But what is chiefly discouraging in it is that in its all too brief entirety it reveals no sense of the dimensions of its subject, contains no hint that culture-identification has been and is still a crucial issue for the Church. The limits of the schema, of course, prevent an exhaustive analysis of Catholicism and culture, but it is hard to take seriously a presentation that ignores the relation of a particular cultural mode to Catholic theology, philosophy, Church administration, liturgical language, ecclesiastical titles, garments and pomp, and even the Church's historic refusals to recognize the autonomy of art, science, and learning. Such failings of omission, probably more than commission, are what is wrong with the schema as a whole and prompt harsh criticism from those who are most sympathetic with its tone and apparent purpose.

Some of the Fathers said this schema was too long, others that it was too short, and both views can be justified. If the schema on the Church in the modern world were to accomplish for the Church the rethinking which is needed in this area, it would have to be a massive undertaking, a whole shelf of volumes. But since obviously such volumes will be a long time in the writing, the schema might better have been limited unashamedly.

For the enormity of the task for the Church in relating responsibly to the modern world and its various cultures can hardly be overestimated. First of all, the Church as an institution will have to overcome the habits and attitudes not of a human lifetime but of centuries. If the Church is to get its hands dirty doing work in the world, it will have to learn that life in the world involves doubt, contingency, and failure; and triumphalism, the need always to be right and successful, has been a long ingrained Roman Catholic attitude. The Church, chiefly the clergy, must learn the habit of listening to the secular world and respecting the world's wisdom and the grace of God at work in it. The hierarchical Church will have to put away its authoritarian cast of mind if it is to be accepted fraternally in a secular world which feels self-sufficient and quite independent of religion. The Church must give up its fascination primarily with itself and turn out to the world, which is after all the only reason for its existence. Most of all, it must learn the instinct of love and service in a modern world it has feared and mistrusted. And changes in attitudes and feelings, which is what all these are, will be harder and slower than administrative reform, the establishment of a senate of bishops, liturgical change, or any such specific, external action.

Furthermore, when these prerequisites are accomplished, when the Church in all its members has learned new humility, openness, and selflessness, then the tasks before it will be possible, but the tasks themselves will still remain to be done. "Reform and renewal" in regard to Catholic understanding and practice of the Christian's vocation in the world will mean repairing the neglect, the errors, and the failings of countless generations in the Church, not excluding our own. To begin with, for its mission in the modern world the Church needs not a declaration on just the modern world, but a new theology of the world itself.

Catholics also need a theology of work. As long as I can remember, we have been talking about the need for a new theology of work, and some of us have been groping toward it. But while we have been talking, the nature of work in the West has been changing so radically in today's automated world, and will change so much more in tomorrow's cybernated world, that efforts up to now will have little value. Perhaps what is needed is a theology of technology or cybernetics. And, since we are told that before many years have passed most of what men know as work in the world will have disappeared, we probably need a theology of leisure-work.

The interaction between religion and culture as a whole, which we are only now beginning even to perceive, will have to be faced up to, first, and then subjected to hard theological and ecclesiological study. Differences in understanding of the Church and its mission now being ventilated at the Council have often come down to culture differences between those Fathers whose experience has been in a "Catholic" national milieu and those whose environment has been pluralistic. The irony beyond this is that such conflicts—deep as they are—usually take place within an overarching white Western cultural outlook. African, Asian, and Near Eastern Fathers have occasionally indicated a sense of exclusion from some of the Council documents and proceedings, sometimes betraying irritation but more often showing extraordinary magnanimity and patience. They cannot be asked to be patient forever.

Some Catholics seem to fear, in connection with this problem, that it would be destructive if the Church were to achieve full penetration and reflection not only of the modern world culture but of individual cultures within it. Adopting new modes in the expression of belief, developing liturgy and forms of Church life in accordance with new or different traditions, languages, sets of imagery and ways of thinking and feeling would mean, they argue, changing immutable truths, losing the integrity and uniformity of the Church's teachings and life over the ages. In answer, several comments can be made. First, those who are most anxious about the problem of changelessness in doctrine do not seem to realize that there is not now, and never has been, a formulation of doctrinal truth which has not been to some extent conditioned by the time and culture within which the formulation was made. This is not a new problem, and there is no escape from it.

Second, it should be obvious that it is unreasonable and actually contrary to the Church's universalism—its Catholicism—for it to choose for itself one culture, one experience, one methodology, and one way of feeling over any others in human history. This is not to safeguard eternal truth but to reduce and imprison it. Lastly, however, we can agree that the dangers to the unity of the Church in multiculturalism and historical response are real, and that it would be foolish to pretend otherwise. Yet it seems clear that the dangers must be accepted, neither ignored nor shrunk from, and the effort made to overcome them, if the Church is to speak and act with all men.

These are only a few of the difficulties that the Church must meet *within itself* in order to know what it will mean to play a responsible role in the community of man and his several cultures. But the people of God are to enter this community to serve it, "not to be ministered unto but to minister," which means that they are to take their share, as Christians, in the labor and anguish of this world. What special Christian share will we have to contribute in laboring with the monstrous, seemingly insoluble problems of the modern world—such as nuclear war, overpopulation, poverty, the emerging nations, racial conflict, the deterioration of cities? Secular authorities and institutions have brought intelligence and technical competence to these problems—for which they have accepted responsibility—and have found themselves almost helpless. Christians as often as not have prattled of "just wars" while the strategists calculated hundreds of millions dead, have offered no more than faith in Providence to the starving and desperate, joined in racial segregation, fled the poor in the cities, and brought their ministry to the comfortable suburbs. Not only must this record of irresponsibility be erased, but the Church's technical incompetence must also be overcome before it can even start to give useful service in the world.

Then there are the special problems that exist for the Church in entering into a modern culture which becomes more secularized by the day. The Church must learn to speak the language of modern man, but it is also true that the language of modern man is fast losing the words for the things the Church wants to say to him. It must be acknowledged, too, that the modern world may have outgrown the need it felt for religion when it was, so to speak, more childlike. Modern, secular men are seldom, as the Church often seems to think, secretly yearning for the solace of religion. More often, they are serenely confident and comfortable in what they are sure is the intelligent, mature man's way of life, and if they think of religion at all it is as a whimsical although occasionally troublesome vestige of the past.

All in all, an inventory of the tasks and difficulties before us—if the Church is to "put on the Father's solicitude for all men," as Schema 13 says, and be with them as they actually are, in their own modern cultures—becomes staggering in its enormity. No doubt it was appreciation of this fact which led some of the Fathers of the Council to recommend at the Third Session that Schema 13 be withdrawn, or delayed indefinitely, or delayed for a specified, considerable length of time. My own criticisms of the schema, with this recital of the vast areas of concern not touched on in the section on culture, may suggest that I too think the schema should be dropped, but I do not. For the Catholic bishops of the world to meet over a four-year period in a Council devoted to updating the Church and to say nothing whatever about the needs of the modern world would be shocking and scandalous. Ideally, the Council's study of the Church in the modern world should have been a companion piece to its epochal study on the Church, since they are two halves of the same problem. But failing that, even a not so successful effort is better than none at all.

In fact, it may well be that the very unsatisfactoriness of the draft as introduced last year has had its own particular value. The schema, with all its inadequacies, did provoke the frankest, bravest, most liberating discussion the official Church has ever engaged in on the subject of marriage and birth control, which has for so long been evaded. A forthright consideration of racial discrimination also was stimulated, as were valuable general interventions on the Church in culture. Many of the Fathers who responded to Schema 13 could scarcely have expected that the bold ideas they presented in the *aula* of St. Peter's would be incorporated in the final draft, but they took the opportunity to join with the bishops in dialogue on these subjects, and through the bishops with the whole Church. This is what has made the Council already so powerful in moving the faithful: the extraordinary extent to which it has become a kind of theater for the working out of the Church's mind on the problems before it.

In conclusion, I think all Catholics can give thanks that the schema on the Church in the modern world was attempted, that it was presented to the bishops and accepted in substance, that it occasioned fruitful discussion which is still going on and must continue for years to come. As I write I have no idea what changes are being made in the schema by the Fathers and *periti* responsible, or what its final form and fate will be. If I had been asked, my recommendation would have been that the schema be reduced sharply, especially in its unfortunate sections on specifics. In the end, its most useful function will be in affirming Christ's life in the world, confessing that the Church has failed its Master in regard to the modern world, indicating the scope of the work to be done, and pledging that this work will be carried on.

And if we believe what we have been saying about the whole people of God and the laity's province of special responsibility for the world, it will be then for all of us in the Church to take our share of this joyous burden. For the vocation of men, as the schema says it, is that "they accept God's gifts with thanksgiving, and making God's plan their own, bring forth fruit in every good work, in all things following Christ."

2

The Break
with Platonic Religion

by MICHAEL NOVAK

I

ALBERT CAMUS received the Nobel Prize because his work "illuminated the human conscience in our time." He probably would have been pleased, had he lived, to see the revolution of religious conscience marked by Pope John's *Pacem in Terris* and the new Schema 13 of the Second Vatican Council. For the key word for describing the relation of the Church to the world is no longer power, triumph, or isolation. The key word is service, and the key text from Scripture is the one which tells us that Christ emptied Himself and took on the form of a servant (Phil. 2:7–9). The whole Church acts in the person of Christ, who came in the form of a servant. She wishes to put order into her complex relations to the earthly city in such a way that her service to the free and self-critical conscience will be obvious.[1]

[1] Throughout this paper I paraphrase or quote directly from the conciliar text of 1964. That text is in the process of amendment, and one can detect in it passages not yet influenced by other passages—an intellectual revolution in the formative stage. For Camus' appeal to Catholics, cf. his talk to the Dominicans in *Resistance, Rebellion and Death* (New York: Alfred A. Knopf, 1961), pp. 67–74.

For nearly four centuries, the Roman Catholic Church has not been at the center of human history. For nearly four centuries, the world has defined itself as "enlightened" from the Catholic Church, and the Catholic Church has defined itself by opposition to the modern world. Her art, her social and economic action, her philosophy, and her theology have not been part of the mainstream of modern history; they have flowed in a smaller, specialized, almost sectarian, stream apart.

Why this alienation between the secular world and the Catholic world? One of the many complex cultural forces which brought it about was psychological, or perhaps epistemological. The churchmen of a certain long period visualized their version of reality as "eternal" or "classical." They were unable to forego their attachment to the past and their comfortable present, and so to move onward on the pilgrimage through history to which God has called His people. Socially, economically, politically, morally, philosophically, scientifically, theologically, they hoped to hold history still. By reaction, many men of good will, giving their loyalty to the future rather than to the past or the present, stepped away from the static Church. Churchmen continued to speak the language of the platonists: of the eternal, the immutable, the static essential, the necessary, the pure. They despised, or pretended to despise, the physical, the contingent, the historical, the sociological, the political, the economic; they disdained the dynamism of those historical organisms which have not yet reached their full and essential development, and the probability schemes which indicate that in history events do not occur in a necessary but rather in a statistical pattern of probabilities.[2]

The period in Church history which has lasted throughout the last four hundred years may be called "the Roman period" of the Church. During that time, the favored images of the Church were borrowed from the Holy Roman Empire

[2] Cf. Bernard Lonergan, "Emergent Probability," *Insight* (London: Longmans, Green & Co., 1958).

of the past: vestments, ceremonies, titles, political practices, organizational structures; and the rhetoric of papal and curial statements imitated the styles of the Roman Empire. The key words which churchmen used in describing the Church were power and jurisdiction. The local Italian church predominated in the central institutions of Church polity, and the social and political life of Italy for a long time only slowly entered the modern era.

The very first paragraph of the new document, however, shows a Church anxious again to renew its pilgrimage with men through history. The Church, it says, wishes to share "the joys and sorrows, the hopes and the anxieties" of men who live today. It knows that it has with all men "a common lot in prosperity and adversity, a common heritage of the past, a common struggle for progress." No longer does the Church see itself, therefore, *in opposition to* other men, or bound to one race or language, one nationality or condition, one cultural style. On the contrary, the Second Vatican Council wishes to see all men as members of one family.

Fundamentally, what is at stake is a break with the mystery religions of the ancient Near East, a break with what might be called the platonic view of the world. No longer does the Church see time as a danger, and the things of this world as mere distractions. On the contrary, the Church now sees in time "a sign, a voice." "In the voice of time, therefore, one must listen to the voice of God." No longer does the Church set herself over against modern progress; instead she now praises many things in modern life. "There are many things which the Church views as well conceived and well executed by the men of our time, and most of all the fact that all men are coming to be recognized as members of one family, and are held in equal regard." The Council "rejoices in the progress of the sciences and the arts."

In the light of the wars and the divisions which still divide the family of man, the Council notes that many men are "beginning to question the deeper meaning of human history, especially the meaning of the modern age." The Council "sees in all the variety of events in which the human race is caught up the operation of the divine Spirit. He it is who is directing the scheme of time, ever renewing the face of the earth. . . ."

The Council asks the children of the Church to "do their part in building up a world," that new world which all men hope for, and which is rising upon the rubble of the wars which have characterized our century. The Council invites all men "to question us about the faith that is in us, to consider with us what man is, and what his vocation and duties in this world might be." Believers and nonbelievers are to cooperate "in the building up of a truly fraternal earthly city."

Thus the Council is at last exorcising the platonic religious spirit from her heritage. For centuries she has condemned platonic heresies: Gnosticism, Manichaeanism, Jansenism. Theologically discredited, however, these heresies have thrived culturally, in the attitudes of Catholic peoples. The new Schema 13 at last comes to grips with these cultural heresies. Instead of asking men to flee from their bodies and to flee from the concerns of earth, it is asking them to find God *through* their earthly tasks, in the joy of their complete and full human life. The Council sees that questions "about culture, the state, the progress of science and technology," are crucial to an adequate view of religion. One question underlies these others, "the question of man and his vocation." Who is man? Where, on this earth marked by concrete tunnels, ribbons of highway, bamboo huts, is mankind headed? The Council wishes to explain "how important earthly things are in man's entire vocation."

But if time is the voice of God, so also is every creature, however lowly, however ordinary, in this world of trees, and ocean, and skies, and lovely people. All creatures are very good (Gen. 1:31), and every creature calls man to God (John 1:3; Col. 1:17). Creatures are a kind of language. "In Christ Jesus man can truly hear and understand the language of things," and a man can and must, "even in temporal goods

hear God and glorify Him as the Father." For things lead beyond themselves, and the beauties of a woman's smile, or of a
cold Alpine valley, or of a crowded and busy city, are capable
of stirring in man's heart an echo of the infinite, creative God.
"Man's heart is opened wider and his hope is elevated beyond
the building of an earthly city." The difference between the
view of the Second Vatican Council and that of platonic religion is that the Council does not ask man to find God by
fleeing from the world, but to find God by listening to the
voice of, and learning the language of, the world.

By his life in the world, a man shows "his fidelity to God
and his love for his fellows." Therein he imitates "the Father's
solicitude for all men, even in earthly affairs." Trying to diminish the amount of suffering in the world, and to realize the
possibilities open to men, he imitates the creativity of God. All
creation, moreover, "eagerly longs" to be better than it is, to
be completed, and to receive the final revelation of its meaning. Yet the meaning of history is not the mere unfolding of
history. History is important, but the final revelation will break
in upon it from "outside," in the second coming of the Lord.
The earth strains to reveal Him who will come, but can only
await His coming. Christians must communicate the beginning of their hope in the best way possible, by the scope of
their friendships and the energy of their creative social and
political efforts.

Thus, the Council sees all creation as driving forward to
fulfill its hopes and to realize the good possibilities which open
up before it. But progress is not simple and direct. Countless
good things are lost and perish in the movement of history.
Dark ages occur. It is the task of free men to manifest their
confidence in the power of intelligence, friendship, and creativity, by intervening in history to realize the good that is
possible, and to avoid impending evils. "The complete vocation of men is . . . to accept God's gifts with thanksgiving,
to make the creative intentions of God their own, to bring
forth fruit in every good work." The Council bases itself on ι

Cor. 3:23: "For all things are truly ours, and we are Christ's, and Christ is God's." There is room here for optimism and for pessimism, for the courage of springtime, and for fidelity in the night.

Moreover, the Council sees that men sin not only in their private lives, but also in their social life. It is not enough for man to be privately moral; society must also be moral. Protestant thinkers like Reinhold Niebuhr, in his *Moral Man, Immoral Society*, have stressed this social dimension of evangelical morality. The Council sees that "the doctrines, institutions, and regulation of labor and leisure often . . . debase the boundless desires implanted in the hearts of men into an inordinate craving for earthly possessions." Science and technology, advancing man's control over matter, "are often transformed into cruel tyrants." As John Updike has written, "We in America have from the beginning been cleaving and baring the earth, attacking, reforming the enormity of nature we were given, which we took to be hostile. We have explored, on behalf of all mankind, this paradox: the more matter is outwardly mastered, the more it overwhelms us in our hearts." [3]

Nor is the Council naive. Men are called "to build the earthly city," and their human nature is "the culmination of the work of visible creation, toward which for countless years the earth's evolution was driving." But men often oppose their own intentions to the intentions of God. Sin has "overflowed into the stream of human history," and "man is born not only with an inclination to evil, but also in conditioning and circumstances which favor evil." The Council recalls a basic matter of fact: "Mankind never ceases to see prosperity ruined by injustice, lying and violence." And these evils are not merely the result of the misapplication of social technique. "They arise also from the pride and selfishness of individuals, and from the fact that many individuals share the same vices, and by those vices contaminate their work and the fabric of

[3] *Pigeon Feathers* (New York: Alfred A. Knopf, 1962), p. 248.

society." Sin is not a social accident; "it breaks out from the inmost depths of man" (Jas. 1:14-15). Man, on account of sin, has a double need of God.

Next, the Council makes clear that the two roles of man's vocation—that he seek first the kingdom of God, and that he faithfully build up the earthly city—are not opposed to one another. "For any earthly culture which turns away from God's intentions and God's light is defective." On the other hand, a religious person "unwilling to be of service in the renewal of the world seeks God in vain." Christians are to live in the world, and to work "as brothers with brothers for the building up of the world." Moreover, they practice their love for God not by fleeing from the world, but "by remedying the conditions of human life and by helping their brothers who are suffering." There is in the world much greed, lying, and hatred; thus all the more must brother cooperate with brother in "the building up of a more just and brotherly society." The love of God must be given flesh and become "daily more apparent" on this earth. Men must "be delivered from want and servitude."

A man is not born a man; he must become a man by developing "his knowledge, morality, spirit, all his faculties, in service to the spiritual and temporal communities to which he belongs." Yet, no matter how busy a man becomes in his efforts to build up the earthly city, he ought not to "neglect to give thanks to God, nor to forget how precious it is to know the living God."

Thus, in chapter I of the new document on the Church in the modern world, the Second Vatican Council has made a clear and important break with the medieval, platonic religious tradition. The Council does not oppose man's good to God's good. It does not oppose earth to heaven. Rather, in more biblical terms, it sees history as a place of pilgrimage, hears time as the voice of God, and learns to listen, while using things, to the language of Him who speaks through them and teaches men by means of them.

II

In chapter II, which is entitled "The Church Dedicated to the Service of God and Man," the Council turns still another corner in the history of religion. In trying to define "the multiplicity of mutual relations" of the Church with the world, the Council tries to stress that this relationship is fruitful both for the Church and for the world, "notwithstanding frequent and inevitable disagreements and difficulties." The Council sees that many of these "difficulties" were due to historical misunderstandings; the Church has had to learn by trial and error. The Church, the document points out, "in the course of the centuries and by a variety of experiences, little by little has come to see many things [in its relationship to the world] more clearly."

The Council points out that of all concepts, service best defines the role of the Church in the world. Even "the apostles and their successors" are, no less than the ordinary people of the Church, "made subject to the Spirit of Jesus, who is the real bond among those who believe." Thus, hierarchy and laity are not merely related by the bonds of legal authority and jurisdiction; they are brothers, of one people, both subject to the "Spirit of Jesus." The role of the hierarchy is "to proclaim the Gospel to all peoples, to gather all believers together in a unity of charity, prayer, and thanksgiving, and to teach them to observe all things which the Lord has commanded." The clergy are the servants of the Christian people; last, not first. "The duty of those who govern the Church in Christ's name lies in this, that they continue the work of Him who came to minister, not to be ministered unto."

The Council next tries to point out that the power of the Gospels is often "shown in the weakness of its witnesses." The Christian religion endures in history, not because its teachers and its people are especially talented, or virtuous, or in any way superior; on the contrary, they are the weak and the poor things of this earth. In their weakness, the power of the Gospels is made manifest. That power comes from God, and not from human talent or intelligence.

The Church, too, the Council points out, is in a sense materialistic; the Church, too, uses temporal things. "Yet she places no hope in the privileges offered to her by civil authority. Indeed, she will gladly renounce the exercise of certain legitimately acquired rights, as soon as it becomes evident that by the use of them, on account of new circumstances, the sincerity of her witness is being called into doubt." With this sentence, the Council pledges itself to break those ties with the secularism of the past, and to resume its pilgrimage in history according to the demands of the historical present. The Church is not an eternal form, always the same in all places, and interested in securing temporal power according to the image of the secular powers of the past. On the contrary, the Church asks one thing: ". . . to be able to preach the faith freely, and to carry out her duty among men without hindrance, using therein all the means that are in keeping with the Gospel and the welfare of men, according to the differences of time and circumstances." It is illegitimate for critics of the Church to judge her according to a platonic standard, insisting that what she has once been she must always necessarily be. For the Church is hereby committing herself to history, emphasizing her concentration upon fidelity to the Gospels, and expressing her willingness to prove her sincerity by her deeds.

"The Church has foremost at heart, with the help of all men of good will, the promotion of true freedom of spirit, excluding any kind of force that may be offensive to the dignity of the human person or corrupt the good conscience. The Gospel wishes to call forth a free response from men, by no means aims at a purely external assent, but on the contrary demands a sincere internal conversion." Thus, the pledge of religious liberty is repeated, which another document of the Council will elaborate more extensively.

The Council goes on to say that the authorities in the spiritual and the temporal orders "must be kept distinct." It is not the duty of churchmen, it stresses, "to interfere in temporal affairs as such. Just as our Lord declined the role of arbiter in earthly disputes and did not allow Himself to be proclaimed king, likewise the pastors of the Church will leave to men the handling of worldly business." The clergy "must be intent only on serving God and the salvation of men, and must never be misled by any desire for domination." On the other hand, they are not to "overlook the fact that temporal affairs, too, are subject to God and the wisdom of His laws, which bind consciences." The Council hopes that "with the aid of divine Providence, in new world conditions, pastors of the Church will gradually be less involved in attending to temporal affairs" and "not inject themselves into the proper sphere of the civil authority." Another corner of history is here rounded.

Next, the Council stresses the fact that the Church is greatly helped by every step of human progress. "Nothing good or true is foreign to the Church, or a matter of indifference." The progress of the sciences, the experience of history, and the riches stored in different cultures allow the nature of man to be better recognized, and bring into view the countless ways by which men are brought to the truth. "All these things increase our awe of God." The growth of human experience and the sciences stimulate the Church in investigating the Gospels more deeply, and in understanding, propounding, and clarifying her own teaching. The criticisms of those outside the Church, even of those who despise the Church, are helpful to the Gospels. "With simplicity of spirit, the Church listens to those who throw up to her the sins of her members and their lack of the spirit of the Gospels. . . . She realizes that she is made up of men, whose fidelity to the impulses of the Spirit is often impeded by their ignorance and their sins . . . a continual renewal is obligatory upon her."

On the other hand, the Church helps in the building up of

the earthly city. The words of God stimulate the life of the spirit, and lead men to strive for love, friendship, justice, freedom, creativity. Those who are faithful to these values, because they believe in God and in Jesus Christ, help to diminish the amount of suffering in the world. The Gospels nourish them in "the difficult struggle against falsehood and injustice," and set before them the goals of a perfect, self-critical and liberating love. Using their intelligence in the light of this goal, "competent men may seek ever better practical solutions." Such a goal is, in Reinhold Niebuhr's words, an "impossible possibility," which sheds prophetic and critical light on every temporal achievement.

The Council recognizes that the Church has no automatic solution for social problems. Unchangingly, she can propose the goal of a charity which no historical form can quite satisfy. But otherwise the people of God have got to use their practical intelligence on immediate concrete problems as intensively as anybody else; and they learn only by trial and error. "But if the Word of God always and changelessly points out the perfect goal of charity in justice and justice in charity, the people of God in feeling their way toward this goal, especially in times of sudden and profound changes, must constantly examine what it is the signs of the time demand." The intelligence of pastors, of faithful, and of those outside the Church must for wisdom's sake be consulted.

The Council warns the faithful "not to think that their pastors are either competent or called to give them an answer to all questions, even serious ones, and tell them what has to be done here and now." The text goes on: "Not surprisingly, the Church's magisterium, in new and difficult questions where there is the matter of applying the principles of current teaching to changed conditions of life, does not immediately have prompt and ready answers or solutions" to all questions. If the faithful cannot wait for a decision from the Church, and must act, "let them be bold enough on their own responsibility to take matters into their own hands according to the dictates of their own conscience, guided always by the Christian prudence [practical wisdom] that is inherent in the truths of the Gospel and in the moral teaching of the Church. Such a conscience, the text states, "always takes note of the individual circumstance in which one must act . . . and of the human sciences that have a bearing on the several problems." Disagreements, the Council notes, will often arise. And the Council suggests as a rule of thumb the phrase of St. Augustine: unity in doctrines definitively proposed, in others free inquiry and difference of opinion, but in all things charity and the humble search for God's will.

Chapter II concludes by noting that the Church must not only teach but also do. There is perhaps a note of boastfulness in this last paragraph. The text asserts that in the course of the centuries, "many Christians have been moved humbly to devote themselves to the service of those who are the poorest, the most abandoned and despised of men. . . . Thus the Church, regardless of the weakness and deplorable disagreements that are found in her bosom, still presents to the world countless examples of genuinely fraternal life." True enough, but only half the truth; a note of sorrow could also be inserted, concerning the selfishness, greed and love of domination which have characterized many clerics and laymen in the long history of the Church, and which lead men to disbelieve in her and her sincerity.

III

Despite its weaknesses, this new document has paragraph by paragraph worked out a historically original and fruitful expression of the genius of the Christian Gospels. The platonic myths in which the message of the Gospels was cast for so many centuries did not do justice either to the emphasis of the Gospels on the Incarnation, nor to their emphasis on man's pilgrimage through history toward the second coming of Christ. The platonic approach to Christianity emphasized, instead, an "eternal" point of view, a changeless "heart of the matter," and it disdained history. The new text relinquishes such Olympian pretensions.

Serious questions, however, are raised by the new approach. What is the relationship between the Second Coming and present history? Most Christians may now agree that the platonic dualism of the eternal versus the temporal is not an accurate vehicle of the Gospel message; but the newly recovered vision which supplants Western platonism, the tension between eschatology and history, needs to be thought out in detail. In the light of the Second Coming, a man can live as a good Christian under Nazism, Communism, or welfare capitalism. But clearly there are moral—and Catholic—descriminations to be made on such social and historical matters. If there is no such thing as a platonic, eternal "natural law," still the experience of human history makes plain that some social systems, some ethical practices, some policies of behavior favor, and others speedily corrupt, human dignity and moral progress. Democracy, for example, as Winston Churchill once said, is the worst of all forms of government, except the other forms; no platonic form of good government, only long human experience, guides our concrete ethical practices. Human wisdom gradually leads to safeguards against recurrent human proclivities to evil, safeguards which do not at the same time destroy the possibilities for good also inherent in human freedom. A nice balance between the known tendencies of men, the circumstances of time and place, and the demands of the vision of Christ's coming kingdom is not easy to strike. An ethic of historical discrimination is one of the first orders of business for the renewed and reformed Catholic Church. The platonic version of the natural law ethic, typical of scholastic textbooks, is not only useless but misleading; a more historical version is seriously needed.

There is also another major undeveloped point in the present text: the distinction between the role of the priest and that of the layman vis-à-vis the Gospels. The text wishes to make clear that the ordained ministers of the Church have a special role in announcing the Gospels, and describes the role of laymen as that of making practical suggestions or speaking from their own concrete experience. But this division of labor between clergy and laymen does not describe the reality. For, in the first place, the ordained priest is often a man of acute practicality and great concrete experience. And, in the second place, it sometimes happens that a layman who has long meditated on the Gospels penetrates to their meaning, in relation to a certain question of human history, to a depth which is not exceeded by any of the priests or bishops of his time. Thus it seems that sometimes laymen have a role in articulating the meaning of the Gospels for their time, while priests rather than laymen suggest new applications and concrete initiatives.

It may well be that the Holy Spirit at a given time or in a given place will speak principally or most clearly through some layman or group of laymen of His choice. For example, it is striking to note the immense impact which Graham Greene, Jacques Maritain, François Mauriac, Gabriel Marcel, and others have had on the spiritual life of a whole generation of laymen and clerics.[4] Often, it is laymen, as Pope John noted in *Pacem in Terris*, who first give rise to the teaching of the Church. It is conceivable that not only in social and political matters, but even in theological and doctrinal matters, it would be a layman who would best penetrate and best express the meaning of the Gospels on a certain point. The distinction between pastor and layman is not based, then, on a distinction between the meaning or the teaching of doctrine and its concrete application. It is rather a distinction between those who have the office to pronounce the *official* teaching of the Church, and those who merely seek to penetrate, discover, or articulate that teaching. Laymen have sometimes been teachers of the *official* teachers.

The clergy have an institutional ministry. Both pastor and

[4] Cf. the autobiographical essays in *The Generation of the Third Eye*, Daniel Callahan, ed. (New York: Sheed & Ward, 1965).

layman are subject to the same Spirit of Christ. Both receive whatever authority they have from the presence of the Holy Spirit in their minds and hearts. What distinguishes them is that only the priest wears the stole, only he makes the institutional decisions between alternative interpretations of the meaning of the Gospels. Laymen, too, may be a source of Christian doctrine, and the harbingers of doctrinal development. But it is not they who have the gift of the Holy Spirit for pronouncing officially whether this, or that, is to be accepted as "the official teaching of the Church."

In this way, priests and laymen are seen to be more nearly brothers than the text has yet expressed. Not only are both equally called by the same God, and equally subject to the same Spirit, but both are called upon to penetrate to their utmost the meaning of the Gospels, and to listen with attuned sensibilities to the voice of their time. Both are called upon to reflect upon the Gospels and upon the concrete experiences of their time. Both are equally involved in a common pilgrimage through the risks and contingencies of history. But to one belongs the office of formal teaching, and the leadership of the eucharistic community, while of the other a less formalized role, a less institutionalized service, is demanded. The Church is in the world institutionally through the priest in the world, and less formally, more variously, through the layman in the world.

3

Man's Social Relationships
to a Changing World

by DONALD QUINN

SCHEMA 13, on the Church in the modern world, is the unique experiment of a unique Church Council. Past Councils have avoided confrontations with the world—at least the worldly world—while Vatican Council II came to the conclusion that it must meet the world head on. In this day the Church has hammered out a social doctrine; the world's own headlong thrust into solution, improvement and progress has established a certain pattern. In fact, the day is upon us when it is apparent that socialization is the format of the future. Really, there is very little else to do but to attempt to establish a dialogue between the world and the spiritual force of Christianity.

Fortunately, the thought of the Catholic Church was ready to work on such a schema as 13. Developments in recent years have brought us to this stage. To mention only two: we would have to look at the development of social doctrine and the

surging force of Teilhardism—which, whether it is acknowledged or not, is forcing itself upon us from many directions.
As to the social doctrine, we have of course the succession of
social encyclicals from Leo XIII's 1891 *Rerum Novarum* to
John XXIII's *Mater et Magistra* and *Pacem in Terris*. To the
encyclicals themselves has been added the work of the Church
in teaching those encyclicals, and so we have developed a long
shelf of knowledge and principles that can be classified as
social doctrine. Meanwhile we have fashioned a great understanding of what can be called the social apostolate—again
stemming in part from the social encyclicals themselves. Reality has forced us to turn our eyes, as they say, toward the
market place and we have even structured a new technique of
"look, judge, and act" to cope with the social apostolate challenge. These things have given the Church some readiness to
enter into the dialogue with the world. At the same time, we
should not fail to stress that we have developed a new dimension of understanding about the world. I would trace this
awareness to the work of Teilhard de Chardin and the
movement which his studies have spurred in the Church. (This
is not to overlook this same kind of movement outside the
Church, and how it has affected us, finally, in these days when
others' ideas can safely be utilized by Catholics.) This Teilhard movement has provided a synthesis that gives the Church
a confidence that it has something meaningful and important
to say to man at this moment of history.

At a time when something needs to be said, this is indeed
fortunate.

Schema 13, in its concept and in its writing, is rather like an
attempt to write a new social encyclical. This "encyclical,"
though, is being written not by the Holy Father, alone or with
his selected advisers, but by all the Fathers of the full Council.
It would not be too much to say that it is really being written
by the world to which it speaks.

Although others may disagree, particularly those who are

not Catholics and who fail to sense the impact of some of the other important work of Vatican Council II, the schema on the Church in the modern world is not the most important fruit of this Council. *De Ecclesia,* for instance, promulgated at the conclusion of the Third Session in the fall of 1964, defines the Catholic Church in such a way that this constitution on the nature of the Church must be recognized as the greatest and most significant accomplishment of Vatican II. Other documents, perhaps with the exception of the ill-conceived decree on communications, each testify to germane work of Vatican Council II. But then, all these deal with "churchy" subjects, all of them treating of those things that are meant to accomplish a pastoral renewal and reform of the Church's very life. In recognition of that fact, it is easy to see why those not of the Roman Catholic allegiance do not put as much stock in them as do Catholics. Instead, they look to the Council's work that deals with the rest of the world—and that means Schema 13.

Schema 13 deals with the Church too, but it is in a different way. It deals with the Holy City. It calls upon the Christian to take account of all that is going on about him. But what the schema cannot do is to frame definite answers to all the world's problems. And, of course, it should not. Perhaps the greatest hazard in its conception and writing was to achieve that delicate balance between speaking in generalities—which would have been meaningless and a disgrace, and would have given absolutely nothing to the world to which it was addressed—and in getting caught up in specific solutions and answers, as if the world it was talking about was going to be set in concrete from that moment on.

The world won't stand still. In a sense, Schema 13 will begin to be out of date from the day it is finally voted. But until another Church Council takes on the same immense task, its guidelines must represent a masterful recognition and encounter of the Church and the World.

This schema, above all, is an appreciation of the Incarna-

tion. It shouts over all that Christ has come to save not merely
the soul of man, but all five feet, eleven-and-a-half inches of
him—him with his six kids and their tuition bills, him with his
ward politics, him with his Rotary button and his union card,
him with his awful nuclear power, him and the world with
him.

The whole world of man, in all of its specialized intricacies,
is almost too much to cope with. The forces of science, technology, human relations, speeding along as they have done
these past few years, have almost swept man off his feet. The
so-called Third Revolution of cyberculture is only one of the
difficult problems. While man's agricultural revolution crept
along for two thousand years and the industrial revolution
loped for two hundred years, the revolution brought on by
automation and computers is coming to full power in something like twenty years. In that short two decades man and
his societies and their governments will have to sort out such
concepts as the difference between leisure, which might be
called a positive and active state that gives man freedom essential for his humanity, and idleness or unemployment, a negative state of nonactivity and nonincome.

So just as soon as we begin grasping the immense proportions of the social and economic conflicts of discrimination,
poverty, unemployment, and the like, we are pushed on to
consider an entirely new idea that, in the old scheme of things,
threatens us. People are still demanding that there be developed a theology of work, how to approach it and especially
how to distribute its products and share its profits. Suddenly,
while we are contemplating *that*, we are called on to develop
a new theology—a theology of leisure.

Such is the challenge of Schema 13, throughout the whole
document and especially in the content of chapter III, dealing
with the social aspects of man. Titled "The Conduct of Christians in the World in Which They Live" when it was presented to the Council Fathers in the Third Session, this third
chapter introduced itself by asking man to cooperate gener-

ously in "rightly building up the earthly city." This is the will of God, said the introduction, that every man use his time on earth "not only to restore his own life in Christ, but also, in the same spirit, to assume his duties in all the communities of which he is a member" (article 15). The will of God, understood the way I understand it—that is, in the spirit of freedom, the will of God represented to man as many possibilities and many opportunities to do that will in different ways, rather than as God's predetermined plan for him—such a will of God is a new and exciting charge put to the Christian. Not only his own salvation, but the salvation of all man's communities, is the object of the witness and service of man.

With such an understanding, Thomas à Kempis would no longer reign as the supreme guide for Christian living.

The developments of the postwar world have brought the Church to grips with the social inclinations of mankind. Meeting these conditions, the Church herself has seen refinements of her own *magisterium*. Two such developments have been suggested: one is the depth thought which dwells on the human character and the meaning of man's encounters; the other is the more popular presentation and scholarly synthesis of the Church's social doctrine as found especially and most recently in *Mater et Magistra* and *Pacem in Terris*, those two grand testaments of the late Pope John XXIII.

If nothing else, John's canonization of the concept of "socialization" in *Mater et Magistra* adds a great deal to the common man's understanding of social teaching. He wrote: "Clearly, social action . . . makes it possible for the individual to satisfy many of his personal rights, especially those of economic and social life; these relate, for example, to the minimum necessities of human life, to health services, to the broadening and deepening of elementary education, to a more fitting training in skills, to housing, to labor, to suitable leisure and recreation. In addition, through the ever more perfect organization of modern means for the diffusion of thought—

press, cinema, radio, television—individuals are enabled to take part in human events on a world-wide scale.

"But as these various forms of association are multiplied and daily extended, it also happens that in many areas of activity, rules and laws controlling and determining relationships of citizens are multiplied. As a consequence, opportunity for free action by individuals is restricted within narrower limits. Methods are often used, procedures are adopted, and an atmosphere develops wherein it becomes difficult for one to make decisions independently of outside influences, to do anything on his own initiative, to carry out in a fitting way his rights and duties, and to fully develop and perfect his personality. Will men, perhaps, then become automatons, and cease to be personally responsible, as these social relationships multiply more and more? It is a question which must be answered negatively."

Socialization, John wrote, is not forced on man from the outside or by forces beyond his control, nor by conspiracies devised either by the devil or by his fellow man. Instead, it is the creation of man answering the needs of his own time and his own place.

Socialization, therefore, demands freedom. Its real contribution is to the fulfillment of human persons; consequently, it cannot be said to be opposed to personalization. If it needs to be said here, and it may indeed, let us understand that by socialization we do not mean Socialism with a capital "S." It might be said, however, as it was often hinted in the Council hall during debates on Schema 13, that socialization would not find an incompatible breeding ground in a sort of Christian communitarianism.

As Pope John pointed out, socialization is basically man's achievement. It has developed coincidentally with all the technical, mechanical, and scientific advances of our age: nuclear power, synthetic chemistry, agricultural modernization, electronics, expanded transportation and communications networks and techniques, and an increase in productivity.

Mater et Magistra contends that socialization is a world socio-cultural process and not merely a new legislative or juridical form. What those paragraphs of Schema 13 dealing with man's social relationships mean, is that man is to understand and realize his worth in the midst of the socialization phenomena. Socialization, in fact, will make more demands on free men as the process and men develop. In this, the challenge put to man in the modern world is not unlike the challenge of the entire *aggiornamento* to the typical Christian life. Who would say that the post-Conciliar Catholicism or Christianity can ever be the same as it was before; that it can ever accept so complacently the notion of faith it accepted for centuries? The obvious answer is that it cannot, and the ultimate result is bound to be a better Catholicism or Christianity than there was before.

The new challenge of responsibility, of freedom from authoritative legalisms for legalism's sake, is only one instance. The post-Conciliar Church is going to force us into taking that responsibility, and when it does we will be the better, the Church will be the better, and Christ will be served the better for it.

So, too, the modern world and its problems and potentials, more deeply understood by man who contemplates it all in a true sense of the Incarnation and of his own vast abilities for free responsibility, or responsible freedom, creates a soaring goal for his fulfillment. These are not idle words, as loaded as they may be with the clichés of the moment. They are more than that because they express mankind's reason for existence.

The progress of the world and the growth of man's understanding of its needs have developed at a time when man has also discovered his own growth in human nature. It is not necessary to point out that these two parallel understandings come, for most Catholics, out of the same Church Council.

One problem with Schema 13, one that the Fathers must surely overcome in the final document, is that it needs to be truly world-wide in its development, its meaning, and its manifestation. If it is not, it will be held empty, and rightly so, by a great majority of the world it is addressed to. In its first draft it was too Western, even too European.

This group of essays is perhaps bound to suffer from the same sterile effect, probably by being too American. But for American readers and American understanding, certainly the target of this group of papers, it is worthwhile at least to look at Schema 13's subject matter in that light. Others can and probably are providing the outlook from other points of view in their own parts of the world. Meanwhile we must fervently hope that the world-wide make-up of the Council's commissions and the full assemblage in St. Peter's will impress on Vatican II the obvious necessity to have, above all, a world-view for this document.

One of the primary conditions which the schema itself places on the problems of social relationships is charity. It is precisely the place to start, provided that we can be rid of some old ideas about charity and substitute for these a charity that can be understood and expressed in its true, *loving* sense. It may be difficult to put aside antique notions that charity seems to raise in all of us, if we deal with the matter at all. Charity should hold great meaning for the Christian because it should, in that sense of love, be the basis of his whole life. In the present it is sometimes hard to believe that charity means much for men, when it should mean everything—not just for their own growth but as the dominant means of preparing the world for the second coming of Christ.

Charity, too, can be embraced by the nonbelieving world in its humanitarian sense; this, after all, produces an end response not unlike the one derived from Christian understanding. Charity, or love, need not carry the stigma of being part of organized, institutional religion if one does not care to view it that way. It is certainly the basis for Christian renewal, but it is the basis for secular renewal too. What is required is a new understanding and a new grasp of it—anything but the dusty and dingy idea of charity that makes one think of an old brick building housing an orphans' home or a poorhouse, or a charity that fancies itself as Christ in giving away a bag of old shoes and clothes or a basket of Thanksgiving food.

We know Schema 13 must speak to the whole world and to all of its people. There is no surer foundation than this spirit of love which can be known to all men. One of the architects of the schema, Bishop Marco G. McGrath of Santiago de Veraguas, Panama, proposed that the aim of the schema be to speak to everybody. He said: "It will surely speak to Catholics. But it is also meant to speak to all those who have faith in Christ. If they don't have that, then it is meant to speak to those who have faith in God. And if they have nothing else but faith in humanity, then the schema will speak to them too."

In its discussion of charity the schema is laying a foundation for the social encounter with mankind. Oftentimes these encounters are governed by justice, but charity is of the utmost importance to the well-being of human relationships. It is the virtue that brings along with it good will and interest and not merely the satisfaction of what is owed. It is hard to see in some of the solutions proposed by Christians that the notion of charity has ever taken hold. Is charity recognized by men, or even Christians, as an absolute necessity? Few of us think that we can assume too much here; we cannot assume that Christians who know the importance attached to "the greatest of these" virtues follow that teaching in all of their affairs. We would say at once that they would change the world if they did. Of course, we have to admit that men do not follow this guide, even though it has been taught in various forms by all ethics and moralities and religions. But at least we must stress that the Church at this time has again to attempt to make love the preamble for man's social relationships. At least in this regard, there is one more chance for Christianity to prove itself.

Schema 13 has another fundamental objective. It is to praise and set before men's eyes the idea of the spirit of poverty. If it is understood and accepted that by this spirit of poverty the

Church is not once again stating the "go sell what you have" line, but rather a reality that exists in selflessness, then this, too, must be a meaningful prelude to satisfactory social relationships.

It is perhaps putting the cart before the horse to try to instill in people such a spirit of poverty for its own sake; deep down such a notion is frightening to many. They think that what is called for is a rejection of the "good life," and they wonder if they are up to it. To understand, instead, that it is possible for them still to take "delight in things," as the schema draft proposes, is another notion, one presenting a somewhat new approach to poverty by the stern and rigoristic Church. It is the experience of people that they don't or won't care so much about material things once they are sincerely committed to a set of loving ideals. It is perhaps a mistake to make such an important point of the spirit of poverty in a schema which is at least trying to give the materially poor of the world encouragement and to assure them that their lot is not one they must always endure.

A third major condition for the encounter of the Church and the world is the desirability of forming a sound public opinion. It is in this final major area that the Church itself can learn so much from the world and can indeed engage in the best kind of dialogue by opening its own ears. *De Ecclesia* has given to the people of God a charter and mandate for acting as full-fledged members of the Church. In one way *De Ecclesia* relied heavily on the development and use of public opinion in the Church. Likewise Schema 13 presents the need for public opinion "especially in matters that concern the welfare of the family and of the whole of society," and makes reference to the salutary influence of mass media of communication.

This disposition to recognize the importance of public opinion cannot be overemphasized, nor overpraised. Needless to say, it is a new idea for the Church. And the Church, in "consecrating" it in a document intended to be a dialogue with the world, shows acceptance of a procedure that is already quite commonplace in many of mankind's dealings, and gives further evidence that the Church herself could benefit greatly from public opinion as it might be stated and transmitted by even lowly members in the hierarchical structure of Catholicism. Upon this idea is based all of those magnificent notions of freedom and honesty in men's dealings with each other—whether the men happen to be the governed and the governors or the shepherds and the flock. In the recent history of the Church it has been shown in more than one instance that the charisms of the Holy Spirit can manifest themselves in all states of life. For the first time in modern times the Church is beginning to grasp this important concept.

The problem of public opinion within the Church is a distinct one from public opinion as it is discussed in Schema 13. The absence of opinion processes is one of the foremost problems of the institutional Church, and is one area in which the Church could benefit from the example of the world. The nurturing of public opinion among the people of God, and the acceptance of it as it develops, will be a tiresome and, in some respects, even dangerous endeavor. However, because the matter poses difficulties is not to excuse its undertaking. Since the days of Pope John, the Church has begun to see that all matters of concern must be discussed openly, with full facts on the table, before they can be understood in their total context and before they can adequately serve the Church. The Church must push on here ever more courageously. In the process of open exploration, I think it safe to say that the hierarchy in many instances is going to discover that there exists a body of opinion quite contrary to their common suppositions.

An example is found in a very simple case. The movement toward use of the vernacular in the Church's liturgy underwent a great transformation in the brief span of a few years. In 1961, shortly before the opening of Vatican Council II, petitions were circulated during the national Liturgical Week within the Church and throughout the world. In article 17, which proposes to discuss the building up of a fraternal community, the draft schema says: "If one wants to make a really valuable contribution toward the building up of a fraternal city, Christians will be mindful of the basic conditions for fruitful activity and for a *genuinely open mind:* the consequences of Christ crucified in the spirit of poverty."

Besides recalling the ideas of Teilhard de Chardin, this particular section touches on the most important and basic notion of the "open mind." The problem of the open mind appears to be almost the curse of any transition generation. Already the experiences, if not traumas, of the *aggiornamento* have brought many in the Church to face this delicate and crucial problem. The world itself has its problem with the open mind. What, after all, is the advantage of having an open mind? How does one open up one's mind? If people could understand more about the why and the how of this openness, if they could be made to realize the meaning of the Incarnation which reveals man and man's institutions as always changing and always developing, then there might be a greater understanding—and more important, a desire—for openness.

One needs only to think of all those persons who have not a single doubt about their good faith but who have minds in concrete. Those persons need help. The very first surprise that faces them is to realize how incompatible is this state of rigidity with the spirit of Christ.

The Church has not done much in past centuries, or even in recent days, to instill in her own people a desire for open-mindedness. This does not take into account the even more depressing thought that the Church has not presented in recent centuries a face of openness to the world outside the Church; it is this world outside which Schema 13 proposes to address, and unless a sincere statement on openness can be set down the effects of this entire project will be much less than anyone will be impressed by.

To discover the signs of the times, which Schema 13 ordains, is exactly what we have failed to do for so long. Sociologists like Abbé François Houtart seem to be quite able to stand apart from their age and to size it up. The rest of us usually wait for the historians to interpret what has happened; by the time they do, it is entirely too late to do anything about our times.

We have good instruction that the Holy Spirit can be of greater help than we have perhaps been willing to let Him be. Certainly, it can be said of men within the Church as well as outside that we do not listen to our own prophets. Perhaps man would be well advised to listen more to hear whatever, and however softly, the Holy Spirit speaks and through whom. At least in the understanding of the signs of the times as put forward by Schema 13, we can take hope that there is an emphasis on the contemporaneity of the Church.

One notion of this is carried in the disturbingly legalistic section which covers such problems as associations with other men. The schema, following the principles laid down in the social encyclicals of recent history, blesses the notion that man must cooperate with other men, and as a matter of fact can profit from such association in various professional, labor, technical, or even international associations. The cooperation, for instance, of professional people or of members of learned societies, are for the benefit of all men—not only Christians. Besides bringing us out of our siege mentality, and exposing us to the ideas of other men, there are the recognized benefits of association in order to get things accomplished.

Not to be overlooked in such cooperation are the international associations. The United Nations and subsidiary international agencies such as the International Labor Organization (ILO), World Health Organization (WHO), Food and Agriculture Organization (FAO), the United Nations Educational, Scientific, and Cultural Organization (UNESCO) are examples of these.

In short, the mandate to Christians in the Church cannot be

better put than it is in a paragraph of one of the finest articles of the schema. Article 20, on the dignity of the human person, a scripturally based and expressive section, ends with this admonition:

"Let the faithful, therefore, not only themselves vindicate the freedom and the responsibility of the human person *by any means and action whatever*, chiefly by changing the conditions of life, but let them also promote the initiatives of others in this matter, whatever they may be, casting aside all mental anguish and pessimism." (*Italics mine.*)

This is, beyond any doubt, the strongest call for action of any Church document in centuries.

"Changing the conditions of life" opens up another idea which will benefit the Church and the world in this beginning of dialogue. Take one instance:

In the consideration of one of man's most pressing problems, cybernation and the effect on work and leisure which this new development brings, there are four major propositions which are central but which are disputed by experts in the field. First, the over-all rate of technical change in the world is accelerating; it is not simply increasing, but the rate itself is growing at a faster pace year by year. Second, it is considered that increases in the aggregate demand will provide adequate adjustment to technological change. This idea is a hopeful sign that men in fully developed nations will not be swallowed up by increased scientific improvements. Third, although often challenged, there is a substantial body of evidence that automation will actually produce more jobs in the long run. This does not mean that problems do not exist all along the way. In the present stage of development it can indeed be shown that automation produces more jobs, but they are new jobs which take entirely new and more sophisticated skills than the ones they replace; therefore they are not jobs waiting to be filled by those workers who are being displaced by automation. A fourth disputed proposition is based on the

assumption that educational requirements are rising more rapidly than is educational attainment.

United States Secretary of Labor Willard W. Wirtz emphasized recently that it is critically important to keep in mind
that *man* not *power* is the end purpose for the solutions of
manpower problems in a developed nation. Himself believing
that automation makes more jobs than it destroys, Secretary
Wirtz nevertheless showed the concern of government offi-
cials when he said: "Unemployment unquestionably affects
the family structure; and the converse is equally true. Responsible, informed parenthood is relevant in any consideration of
a responsible, informed position regarding manpower supply
and demand." The Secretary lamented that "in the public
forum, discussion of one large factor in the manpower area
remains blacked out by a taboo. There is strong indication that
a disproportionate number of the unemployed come from
large families—but we don't pursue the evidence that would
permit either establishing this as a fact or evaluating its significance." So in this one commentary, we have a public official
referring one problem area of Schema 13 to another of the
document's problem areas; surely these matters are tied to one
another.

But the message for the Church is larger than this: In addition to pointing to the need of a joint consideration of both
work and family limitation, this example gives evidence of the
way in which the problems of man and the problems of morality are inevitably bound up. Solutions of human problems are
virtually impossible if the needs of society are not considered,
if they are dismissed as extraneous. Unless man can consider
all the data available to him in arriving at his decisions, he
cannot hope to reach conclusions necessary to his successful
development and progress. Completely separate from the
weighty personal, psychological, conjugal, and biological indications being placed upon the question of family limitation,
then, is the added dimension that requires man to consider
family size in his approach to the public questions of demog-

raphy, immigration, national survival, poverty, food abundance, and work forces.

It is a lesson for the Church to learn, as Schema 13 seems to suggest, that man cannot be considered a moral automaton, with no reference to the life surrounding him. His morality must be somehow influenced by conditions and situations; further, his reason must be allowed to function in order to arrive at satisfactory answers consonant with the Incarnation and Redemption.

When Schema 13 discusses economic and social life, as it does in article 23 of the draft, the Church takes on a meaningful and purposeful stance. Some could criticize such discussions as exceptionally naive; some would say for the Church to propose to the world that all men should, let alone could, love one another, or that all should work for the mutual benefit of the whole, is a Utopian prospect. But after all, is it not what the Church must say when it says anything? Is it not necessary for the Church to exhort us to the fullest sense of love among men, not only for their own individual salvation, but for the universal order of mankind? It is interesting to consider the discussions on the economic and social aspect of world life as positive statements from this encyclical-like document.

The Fathers of the Council take note of the increasing and even "daily more widespread kind of socialization, that is, a variety of mutual influences and mutual dependencies in all economic and social affairs and in the combination of them," as is the current experience of men. It is in this section that Vatican Council II adds its own weight to the social encyclicals of the late Pope John XXIII. Propositions such as this are set forth: "As men gain more and more control over created things . . . the best of men hope for a more humane and social order."

Schema 13 then reiterates those designs of Pope John enunciated in the encyclical *Mater et Magistra*. Among these are *economic development*, which must be controlled by man for the good of all nations, not just the rich ones; *advancement*, so arranged as to benefit all men and groups; *distribution of goods*, which belong to all men and all nations as a common inheritance of the whole human race; safeguarding the *integrity of each nation* of peoples; *profit sharing*—since progress comes from the united action of men "it is unreasonable and unjust to seek that progress by excluding workers, whatever the form of their labor, from receiving a just share in the fruit of their common labor"; and finally the *right of workers* to join in union associations.

On one of those pages debated by the Council Fathers, there is the phrase, "The Church therefore is bound to no particular economic system." The schema, in calling for social and economic forms to be "constantly adapted prudently and boldly to new conditions, so that they will always be in conformity with human nature and the purpose of those goods," is adopting a progressive line which is almost incomprehensible in the day-to-day market place of what is called free enterprise capitalism. The discussion of these concepts brought forward some of the most profound explorations of social justice to be heard in the Council hall.

Such phrases as the "Church has nothing to fear from preaching justice under every form" of economic system were heard. One Father could say "the unequal distribution of riches is among the chief causes of social unrest" in the world. Another, Bernard Cardinal Alfrink of Utrecht, said that the Council could not simply repeat the condemnation of Marxism. "Everyone knows where the Church stands," he said. "Atheistic materialism is either theoretical or practical—and one is no less dangerous than the other." But Bishop Antonio Pildain y Zapiain of the Canary Islands said this: "Some apparently 'Christian' nations are wealthy, while others are deprived of the basic necessities. The remedy is not Communism. The remedy is in 'communitarianism,' a concept based on the Gospel. This spirit provides us with the basic rule that in grave necessity all things are held in common."

4

The Church
and Her People in Community

by JOHN G. DEEDY, JR.

SECTION 16-d of Schema 13 prods the "social nature" of Christians and urges them to "take part in community programs and activities, lending their cooperation also to the renewal of the agencies for cultural, social, and civic activity." It is an extremely brief section and, given the state of affairs, quite superficial. Yet the brevity of treatment attracts rather than discourages comment; because community commitment is basic to meaningful concern with the modern world, we seize upon 16-d as the topic of this essay.

Section 16-d received no great attention from the Council Fathers during Third Session debate on Schema 13. Perhaps some Fathers felt their mind on the matter was made sufficiently clear in the chapter on the laity in *De Ecclesia*, a chapter which alludes several times to the layman's responsibility of engaging in temporal affairs and ordering these according to the plan of God. Perhaps some realized that the subject would (or should) be treated in depth in the pending schema on the lay apostolate, a schema devoted in substantial part to program. Perhaps some considered the issue so obvious and elementary as not to demand more than passive, tacit assent.

A rationale can be advanced for the first two attitudes, but the third (which we suspect might predominate) smacks of condescension on a matter on which the Church can ill afford complaisance. It is all well and good to speak of the layman's obligation to witness in community, but it should also be noted that community demands of the Church a commitment that completely dwarfs the record of the past.

Where to start?

Some months back a release from the Dutch Documentation Center spoke of the strength and the insights which the Church stands to gain through those of her members who are in the forefront of temporal affairs. The observation would be a repetitious truism, except that in recent centuries the Church herself, not just her members, has been more than a little detached from the temporal sphere. Certainly the Catholic Church in America has been. It has been almost as if the temporal was to be shunned (despised even) because, in the end, it was only the eternal that mattered. This situation produced many unhappy consequences, and is partial reason why a Schema 13 is necessary.

One consequence of this detachment (to be a major focus of this essay) was the development in the American Church of an organized lay apostolate which, barring a few exceptions, was so narrow in its outlook, so inbred in its preoccupations as to be a frequent embarrassment to the sensitive and, indeed, an impediment to the witness which Schema 13 encourages. One may make this remark even while admitting that the witness carried into community by lay Catholics has been substantial. This is as *De Ecclesia* says it should be, and as Schema 13 wants it.

In point of fact, this lay witness becomes the more impressive when one considers that in the overwhelming number of cases the roots of the witness have been principally in the interest and dedication of individuals acting out of their own initiative and idealism. The Church, unfortunately, has been less the inspiration in generating commitment to the community than one might think and certainly less than one might hope. One explanation is that the Church's own example of community commitment has been deficient.

This last observation will be challenged by official spokesmen, but we suspect that the intensity of the challenge will be dictated more by instincts to rationalize than by deep conviction that the Church has really discharged duties-in-full in involving herself in community. The evidence that she has not is all around us. One aspect was documented in a 1963 study by Dr. Clifford C. Ham, Jr., assistant professor of urban affairs in the University of Pittsburgh's Graduate School of Public and International Affairs. Dr. Ham found that "the complexities of urban life (read community, since society today is largely urban) have not been fully accepted by the leadership (of the Churches) and so emphasis on individual needs continues to predominate. . . . The Churches as social institutions do not participate directly in decision-making nor in motivating social change."

In one sense the detachment of the institutional Church from community decision-making seems reasonable enough; after all we in America do live under a system of law which separates Church and State and makes the body politic responsible for the governing and, increasingly, the welfare of the people. But in other, more subtle senses, the indictment holds. The Church has stood apart. Archbishop François Marty of Rheims commented in the Third Session debate that if the Church is to be "a leaven in the world," the Church must see the world, and therefore the community, as an important element of its mission. But has the Church always so seen the community?

The Ham study, which dealt with the present and potential

role of the neighborhood church in assisting with the physical and social revitalization of declining communities, gives a localized American answer. It concluded that not the common good, but "self-preservation and the continuity of the religious institution" were apparently the strongest motivations for Church concern with community improvement; it also concluded that "preservation of the organization" was more important to the members thereof than a program of social integration or community development. In other words, the concern of the Church and her members was first for the institution, a curious juxtaposition of values for those who professedly live by and regularly stress the supremacy of the common good.

In the context of a discussion on a conciliar draft text one does not attach absolute significance to a single sociological study. The Ham study, for one thing, is limited. It examines but one area of community life; also, it is confined to only three confessional units (a Jewish synagogue, a Protestant parish and a Catholic parish) in only one U.S. city. Yet patterns are sufficiently clear, so that Dr. Ham's conclusions may be widely projected. Besides there is other testimony. Only recently a California priest wrote despairingly that in the populous, sprawling archdiocese with which he is connected "the voice of the Church is rarely heard" in issues of welfare planning, city planning, public education, and social reform. (He added, though, that it does come through loud and clear where property rights are concerned.)

Restricted in scope though the Ham study might be, it points up a problem that not only transcends denominations but ecclesiastical jurisdictions as well. The communities are precious few in which the functions of the religious organization are seen clearly, understood magnanimously, and selflessly pursued. Too often the Church is disposed to consider her job done when she has sent into the community chaste and pious people intent upon the salvation of their souls. Yet this is only part of her job. As Schema 13 counsels, the Church should fill the community with people anxious "about the spiritual, moral, cultural and material needs of all men, without distinction of race, nationality, or condition." This is true Christlikeness; this is the living of the Word. But it is not the uniform history of the Church in America, past or present.

The tendency of the Church too often has been to glorify her "ideal functions" as an institution and to leave community (except when certain moral sensibilities are outraged—as when a questionable movie comes to town or a novel with four letter words shows up in the public school library)—to the body politic. Under the circumstances, it is not surprising that religion should come to be regarded as "a Sunday sort of thing" and that community should, in turn, come to be considered a political preserve, and nothing for which the churches need have worry or regard.

This situation is perhaps made to order for politicians, but it is less than one would want the Church to be content with. Separation of Church and State in America is a national cornerstone, but separation of Church and State does not preclude the Church from speaking to the community, and infusing community with the moral, cultural, and social values which are uniquely hers; nor does it preclude the Church from sending into community men and women anxious to bring to temporal affairs the fruits of these values. But in effect it has.

Indeed, it is almost as if the Church built her own wall of separation between the City of God and the City of Man. For if the complaint can be made that the State often walls itself off from the Church, it is no less true that in many respects the Church has walled herself off from the State. Within the Catholic Church, seemingly more than other Churches, focus on the City of God has frequently been so exclusive and interest in the City of Man so negative that among huge numbers of believers the City of Man (the community) has come to be regarded as hardly more than the mere sum of bricks and mortar, crimes and corruption, politics and pleasures (most of the latter "temptations" and impediments to salvation).

Imperfectly has the City of Man been seen as a place of people whose transit to the City of God might be facilitated in proportion as the City of Man ennobled and elevated the spirit. The City of Man has been defaulted, unconsciously no doubt, by the very institution that claims to be able to give the most to those who must work out their salvation in that city. It is as though the spiritual needs of believers, presumably to be satisfied completely within the formalism of the ecclesiastical institution, were all that counted, and as though man's physical, psychological, and social needs bore no relation whatsoever.

Yet the fact remains that we are a pilgrim people of a pilgrim Church, and our salvation and the Church's fulfillment are bound up intimately with the manner in which the respective roles in community affairs are met and discharged. A private morality is wonderful, but it must be community-oriented if the Church and her members are to be the leaven of which Archbishop Marty spoke. A ghetto morality is not only inhibiting, it is downright self-defeating.

All of which is to say that it is not enough for the Church in Council merely to address adult man and remind him of the responsibility which is his as a member of the community. The Church must also look to herself and resolve to become a living example of community consciousness and commitment; she must be the quintessence of all that she urges on others. This is not a call for the Church to intrude into government, but it is a reminder that the Church has not exhausted her responsibility to community by the operation of schools and hospitals and the sponsorship of welfare services, vital as all these surely are and important though they be in the total Church-community picture.

There are several avenues for the Church to pursue in refining her commitment to the community. Certainly her pastors should be encouraged to temper preoccupation with the "parish plant" and the "parish family" with a real and meaningful solicitude for the community as a whole; this would include deeds as well as sermons which "pledged" the clergy and the parish in the persons of its priests, and which likewise emphasized to parishioners the obligation of their personal involvement in community affairs. The Church's schools could lay greater stress on the urgency of Christian witness in the temporal realm. The Catholic press could strive to inculcate in its readers a keen sense of community (this to be accomplished not by editorial preachment, but by reportorial evidence that the Catholic press has an interest in news besides that which involves the Church herself). Priests and nuns (nuns especially) could be loosed from rectories and convents in order that they might bring to community more of the benefits of their special vocations. Then there are the associations of Catholic laymen, a source of enormous potential, but as yet not effectively exploited, for community good.

Perhaps the sorriest chapter in the American Church's detachment from community is that her lay associations by and large have been allowed to waste themselves. In her lay groups the Church had an obvious and natural avenue for moving into community, reinforcing moral and social values, and bringing to bear ethical and moral considerations on problems which too frequently are thought of only in their secular dimension. In her lay associations the Church had the opportunity of influencing without intruding clerically, of witnessing to the broad as distinct from the denominational good, of displaying concern for the *whole* man in his *total* situation. Instead the Church permitted her lay groups to become idle, inbred and irrelevant, insensitive to changing times and circumstances, and perpetuators of perhaps once necessary but long since altogether narrow loyalties. There are exceptions to this indictment, notably in social action and race relations groups. But still the charge can be leveled that as they presently exist the so-called lay Catholic Action groups in the United States are more an encumbrance than a resource for the realization of witness in the modern world which Schema 13 seeks.

Catholic lay organizations in the past few years have come

sharply under the microscope of analysis. However, to this point the scrutiny has resulted more from the recently freed impulse to criticize everything in the Church, no matter how sacred, than from any new vision of the challenges confronting the Church or the layman in community. Yet whatever the motivation, since the one is almost inevitably linked to the other anyway, the re-examination is welcome; in fact, it is long overdue.

The first thing that can be said about Catholic lay organizations generally is that they are lacking in purpose and impact; they are uncoordinated and aimless, and they abound in such fantastic multiplicity that they discourage rather than invite the membership of the majority of Catholic laymen, especially the most thoughtful (and, therefore, potentially the most influential). It is not an exaggeration to say that vast numbers of men and women refuse to be called to meeting for no better purpose than to witness an exhibition of gymnastics or sleight of hand, and to hear an insipid talk on table decorating or garden manicuring.

Father Stanley M. Grabowski wrote in the March, 1964, *U. S. Catholic* that he counted over three hundred associations for laymen in the *National Catholic Almanac*, including such stunners as the American Christmas Crib Society, the Raskob Foundation for Catholic Action, the Catholic Petroleum Guild, the Catholic Aviation League of Our Lady of Loretto, the Catholic Institute of the Food Industry, the Catholic International Federation of Physical Education and several score more equally superfluous organizations. One could write a hilarious lampoon of societies such as these, except that the scandal of their multiplicity is so very real.

Some might protest that extreme examples are being cited and that it is unfair to indict all lay groups indiscriminately. The objection has validity. However, value judgments are such within the Church that we suspect that those who object to our charge would exempt from the indictment the very lay associations which we would list within it. For instance, most

U.S. Catholic laymen have been indoctrinated into thinking instinctively of the Holy Name Society as the ideal agency for organized male apostolic activity. Why wouldn't they? They are told regularly from the pulpit that the Holy Name Society is the traditional implementing force for Catholic Action in the United States; they are repeatedly reminded of the papal endorsements of the society (usually by Popes long dead); they are urged not to let pass the society's rich indulgences. All well and good—except that a mere casual study of the lay apostolate exposes the Holy Name Society as among the most outdated of lay associations, indolent to challenges and chained to the past. As recently as February 2, 1964, a parish of our acquaintance, in a bulletin endorsing this "greatest of all societies," listed as the Holy Name Society's five objectives: "(1) to honor the Names of God and of Jesus Christ by the example of a sensible religious life; (2) to spread and increase love for the sacred Name of Jesus Christ; (3) to suppress blasphemy, profane and indecent language; (4) to prevent false oaths in and out of our courts; (5) to impart to Christian men courage in the profession of their faith." These objectives were fine and honorable in a day when cursing and perjury might have been the chief temptations to a Catholic and when the profession of faith did indeed demand courage. But certainly that was another day when another witness entirely was expected of laymen.

Challenges today are so different, so much more subtle, that it might be advisable if everyone faced up to the fact that the Holy Name Society is archaic, and perhaps better off consigned to the pages of history. Actually the handwriting has been on the wall for the Holy Name Society since the American hierarchy opted years ago for a National Council of Catholic Men and established such a department within the National Catholic Welfare Conference, the U.S. bishops' central administrative agency headquartered in Washington, D.C. It is only intransigence and the tendency to perpetuate the past that can account for the lingering on in parish after parish of a society deep in its dotage.

But in refining commitment to community it is not only a question of eliminating the outdated; it is also one of coordinating and consolidating overlapping groups and of updating those lay organizations that have a place, that indeed do fit into the Church-community pattern. By way of example with regard to the latter, even such an enduring association of laymen dealing with a timeless problem, an association such as the Vincent de Paul Society, cannot exempt itself from reappraisal. The Bible tells us that the poor we will always have with us and so the Vincent de Paul Society dispenses its charity. But the Great Society wonders whether, with increased public social and welfare services and government-sponsored wars on poverty, the biblical phrase might be rendered more quaint than prophetic. What is the Vincent de Paul's role in this effort? The point is that as the State more and more broadens health and welfare services to its people, lay agencies in this specialized work must take inventory of themselves. The same holds true for lay associations active in other areas where government is expanding its influence, such as in civil rights and civil liberties.

One difficulty in all of this is the penchant of American lay men and women to compartmentalize—to establish under Church auspices organizations parallel to those which exist in the secular community.

The section of Schema 13 dealing with "the dialogue" for "promoting mutual acquaintance and mutual respect in fraternal communion" (article 18) discourages the multiplication of "temporary institutes" and encourages working within "the limits of one common institution that is in conformity with the principles of Christian doctrine." The context may be different, but the counsel is applicable to any discussion about lay associations. It is silly to set up Catholic Boy and Girl Scout programs, social action societies, and what-have-you to compete (the word is sometimes too exact) with similar, fully meritorious secular associations.

The consequences of such duplication are several. For the Church-related group there is the further withdrawal from community, the possibility of partial witness to a cause, and (in the sponsorship of Scout troops, for instance) the expenditure of funds which frequently can be ill afforded and which not infrequently still results in an inferior program. For the secular group there is the deprival of strength that could be put to better advantage. The whole business is unnatural and not surprisingly sometimes spawns a hostility between the counterpart groups which, if it does not hinder their respective work, often does little to promote community concord.

Worth noting is the example of a ranking official of the Catholic Council on Civil Liberties who recently resigned from that organization because he felt that a "Catholic" organization in the civil liberties area is not a sound idea, the "mainstream" of civil liberties activity being in the American Civil Liberties Union. Now many Catholics are nervous about the American Civil Liberties Union, primarily because the ACLU has not always reacted instinctively as Catholics would have it react in many matters close to the hearts (and the welfare) of Catholics. Nevertheless, to borrow the logic of the resignee, the ACLU is the veteran campaigner for civil liberties in the country, it does have national scope, and it is in the thick of all civil liberties debates. The arguments are powerful for Catholics to bear their civil liberties witness (and bring their positive influence to bear) within an established agency such as the American Civil Liberties Union, rather than to band themselves into a counterpart association which, if one projects the lessons of history, will never amount to much more than a fringe group and which, likely as not, will isolate much of the membership from full and sometimes even meaningful participation in the cause. One says this in full knowledge of the impressive "friend of the court" which the Catholic Council on Civil Liberties was able to be, precisely because it is a Catholic organization (with or without port-folio), when the Connecticut birth-control law was being challenged before the United States Supreme Court in February 1965.

No stronger case can be made for the effectiveness of united, as distinct from individual, denominational witness in behalf of the common good than the National Conference on Religion and Race which, since its founding in Chicago a few years ago, has helped mightily to advance the civil rights cause nationally and to correct social ills locally.

This might sound to some almost like a call for the abolition of Catholic lay associations; it is not. It is only a suggestion 1) that the Catholic witness is sometimes to be better made within a secular group than within a specifically Catholic body; and 2) that whatever else might or might not be the case, coordination and consolidation of Catholic lay associations are urgent. (Pope Paul himself at an audience on February 17, 1965, mentioned the "inefficiency of apostolic works" as one of the "thorns that enter deep into the heart.") Decision as to point 1 can only be made by the individual, taking into consideration his instincts, preferences, and talents (he should, of course, have the encouragement of the Church to reach a decision); point 2 demands some intense and honest organizational soul-searching and a willingness to sublimate vested interests and hallowed traditions for more adroit methods and wider potential.

To achieve desired ends in America, point 2 would seem to require some machinery—in order that associations may be helped in their re-evaluation, counseled in their redirection and, in cases where suppression or disbandment might be in order, so that worthwhile talent might be advantageously rechanneled. The appointment of a commissar or a police-type commissioner for coordinated Catholic Action is not necessary; ends might easily be achieved if all (bishops as well as people) placed in two existing national federations of lay organizations—the National Council of Catholic Men and the

National Council of Catholic Women—a confidence equal to the hope that brought them into being.

The NCCM and the NCCW are not without their faults and their weaknesses (the NCCM right now has a tarnished image for the docile manner in which its executive board knuckled under and allowed a few anonymous bishops to kill a television series on marriage morality prepared by its communications department); even so, the NCCM and the NCCW are full of promise.

The NCCM and the NCCW are not superorganizations; they are in business to act as a clearinghouse for programs, ideas, and techniques. They have a vision of community and the modern world, and they seek to bring the weight of Catholic principles to problems which cry for the attention of committed people. Their aims are high and they would seem to deserve more of an opportunity to synchronize and upgrade lay involvement in social, cultural, and civic movements than some in authority appear willing to impart to them. A February 1965 brochure announced that seventy-three diocesan councils were affiliated with the NCCM. This would mean that almost as many sees are "out" as "in"; there are 148 dioceses and archdioceses in the United States. (From the standpoint of the liturgy alone, how much more desirable than stand-pat Holy Name Unions and parish Holy Name Societies are diocesan and parish Councils of Catholic Men under the wing of a liturgy-conscious NCCM.)

The vesting of absolute and complete faith in the NCCM and the NCCW, and, at the same time, the freeing of the two conferences from the restrictions of institutional authority (perhaps to be best achieved by separating both from the National Catholic Welfare Conference), might be exactly the impetus needed to impel Catholic lay action in the United States to heights long envisioned but never approached. No one is saying that full endorsement and total freedom are the only essentials. But they are prime, and necessary for the displacement of the coffee and cards, beer and pretzels set, with men and women who have a grasp of the problems of the modern world and a desire to do something about them. It is long since time to acknowledge that the lay strength of the Church is not bound up with the men and women who usher at Mass and mend the altar linens, not with the faithful attendees at the Holy Name smokers and Monday night whist parties, not with cafeteria volunteers and hospital aides, good and valuable though these people may be, but rather with men and women in community who may never go near church except on Sunday, but who have brains that think and heads that can store and apply the Church's social doctrine. It is the latter that our lay organizations must reach and mobilize as witnesses.

The problems that cry for the attention of the apostolically formed man and woman are all around us, and they are not the problems of the parish plant. They are the problems of community, of change and upheaval, of revised standards and new values, and they are categorized under such headings as crowded cities, deteriorating neighborhoods, automation, poverty, school drop-outs, youth unemployment, senior citizens, racial discrimination, family disintegration, and delinquency.

It is in the related corrective areas of urban renewal, manpower retraining, education, youth incentive, and the stabilization of the family that the layman must bear his witness, so that programs of justice and opportunity will not be neglected and, more important still, so that once initiated they will be insured dimensions beyond the purely secular and the mere political. It is in these areas that civilization is shaped; the Church through its laity must help in the shaping.

But the Church also has an institutional role in this drama. For her to develop the notion of the responsibility and service in the laity is only to half meet the challenge; she must also rally herself. She must testify to her social solicitude by concrete demonstrations that involve herself as an institution in the very things that her theology preaches.

The Church can do this in different ways, and there is evidence that in some places she is going about the task. An example would be the Diocese of Pittsburgh's open-door admissions policy at schools in depressed neighborhoods and its tutoring projects and study halls in sections where study at home is difficult or impossible. These programs have no religious strings and are totally free of proselytism; they are pure and sincere efforts to contribute to the broad common good irrespective of the faith of the beneficiary. (Also, they were launched by the diocese well before there was any talk in Washington about a war on poverty or an Economic Opportunity Act, a fact which no doubt helps explain the speed and ease with which major phases of the Diocese of Pittsburgh's depressed neighborhoods program became acceptable to the government for financing once the Economic Opportunity Act was a reality.)

It is this sort of community consciousness and institutional commitment that the Church must foster. The Archdiocese of Baltimore has an Inner City Program which joins thirty parishes in confronting the social and religious needs of Baltimore; the Archdiocese of Chicago has a Conservation Council which makes the archdiocese an ally of the city in urban affairs that have a Church-State interrelation. This is the modern Church at work in the modern world. It is precisely where the Church belongs—not, as is too often the case, locked within herself, ministering to personal needs and suffering a civic paralysis. Others should be as progressive as the sees cited.

They must be if Schema 13 is to be all everyone prays it will be—in America and all places else.

5

Marriage and the Family
in a 'New' Society

by SIDNEY CORNELIA CALLAHAN

IN the current renewal of Christianity the Church is asserting its mission to the world. With a new realization that no part of life is outside the Redemption, Christians are attempting to meet the challenges of the world of everyday men with a relevant and dynamic Christian message. One important aspect of the general renewal is a new concern with the theology of marriage, a most relevant matter to the majority of mankind who are, or will be, married. This development of Christian thinking about marriage and the family has been a gradual process but, as with so many other things, the convening of the Ecumenical Council in Rome has crystallized the movement for reform. As the Council is trying to express the new life, vigor and insight of Christianity, it is appropriate that there should be a schema called "The Church in the Modern World," and that it should include a section titled "The Dignity of Matrimony and the Family."

The whole draft of this Schema 13 was debated, but no part received more attention than the section dealing with marriage. Section 21 of the draft schema was widely reported, heatedly argued over, and carefully scrutinized by Council Fathers, theologians, and the knowledgeable laity. Expectations had been aroused; those seeking intellectual and moral guidance looked to the draft schema to see what guidance the Church might give through the Council. What did they find? And even more important, what should be the course of the Church's future teaching about marriage and family life?

Upon examination, the draft schema's section upon the dignity of matrimony and the family provokes a curious reaction: it is both beautiful and disappointing. The beauty resides in its felicitous way of relating truths about the family and marriage to the central Christian truths, but the disappointing qualities of the statement arise from its omissions. Excuses can be made, of course. Given the brevity of the treatment, a certain inadequacy may be inevitable; and there is the fact that marriage is discussed elsewhere in other conciliar statements concerning the nature of the Church and the Sacraments. After all, Schema 13, concerned with the world and addressed to the laity, rightly concentrates its discussion of marriage and the family in relation to society at large. But even with these limited aims more could be said, and hopefully will be said, before the Council closes.

Naturally, over half of this section of the draft devotes itself to a veiled grappling with the problem of birth control. I say "naturally" because with the conditions of turmoil existing within the Church over this issue, a disproportionate concern with contraception mars every discussion of Christian marriage (including this one). But since all of the debate in the Council over this draft section centered upon the allusions to birth control, and since a special papal commission is at present reviewing the Church's teaching, the temptation to have one's say once again is irresistible. Besides this, there is a further justification in the draft schema's own plea for the mar-

ried laity's collaboration in solving their "many conflicts."
But before launching into a cursory critique of the swirl of
theological debate over contraception, there are a few per-
tinent points and comments to be made upon the neglected
first half of the draft dealing with the family.

The draft begins very impressively by asserting that God
has established the order of the family to facilitate the development of the person. It continues with a declaration of the
right of each man to be born into a healthy family, reared in
it, and in good time to establish a family of his own. The nature of the family is called sacred since the individual Christian family is an image of and a participation in the covenant
of love of Christ and the Church. While the family institution
still faces grave dangers, the draft schema rejoices that the
value of the family has been recognized by the world.

Interestingly enough, at an earlier date in history a Christian affirmation of the family as an institution would need to
have been stronger. The early experiments in Communist
Russia, and the fervent socialist founders of the communal
kibbutzim in Israel deliberately weakened the family structure in an attempt to further personal liberty and group progress. However, these experiments were not successful in the
long run; guided by purely pragmatic reasoning the revolutionary societies restored and strengthened the family. Ironically, only China, the land of traditional filial piety, denies
even lip service to the value of the family. Today most of the
world, and certainly most of the free world's experts in psychology and the social sciences, could respond affirmatively to
the Church's claim that the welfare of the human person and
of human society is closely bound up with the welfare of the
family.

Happily, too, the schema gives a new and welcome emphasis
to the relationship of family and society. In the description of
the Christian family's vocation there is the recognition that,
like Christ, the family must turn out to its neighbor, and
actively seek the welfare of the whole environment in which

the family lives. Unfortunately, the individualism and parochialism which for too long has marred Christian thinking has also affected the ideals of the family. The Christian family's social and civic responsibilities in the world have been slighted. Too many Christian families have passed by and ignored the most grave injustices of their society, as long as piety and peace reigned in their own homes and schools. True, the right to give one's children a religious education is important, but the Christian family's social responsibilities extend far beyond obtaining benefits for its own religious communion. Much more than a secluded good example is required of Christians, especially of those Christian families to whom much has been given.

And here, necessarily, begin my negative comments on the draft schema's treatment of the vocation of the family. While everything that was said was excellent, there are a few omitted points which might well strengthen a statement's relevance to our complicated and rapidly changing world. First of all, the question of the differences between families, their members, and their different vocations was not mentioned. I should like to see a recognition that many human talents, gifts, and capabilities cannot be exercised within the family alone. In reality, each adult married person has a double vocation, or a vocation within a vocation—to his family and to the world. The married partake of the multiplicity of gifts, ministries, and ways of serving that characterize the single members of the Mystical Body. With different talents there are different calls to different works; marriage does not absolve one from responsibilities to service. The different responsibilities of husband and wife to the world may affect the decisions and outward form of individual families. There should be a Christian encouragement of variety and individual patterns of family life. Just as there are many different forms of the religious vocation, so there can be differing manifestations of the married laity's Christian commitment.

In particular, the schema's treatment of marriage and the

family might well assert the married woman's Christian responsibility for the Church and the world. Christianity has long championed the freedom, equality and dignity of single women and Religious, but hesitated to affirm the Christian responsibility of married women to develop and use their talents beyond the family. Unfortunately, in the past, custom, culture, and a misguided concern for the family have conspired to keep married women from growing up into the fullness of Christ by confining them to stereotyped roles. But today Christian maturity, initiative, and responsibility must be the goal of every Christian; no one can arbitrarily be assigned passive, subordinate positions. If masculine privilege and dominance have inhibited the opportunities and development of half of the human race, then Christians must lead the way in restoring women's equality, dignity, and development. Those Council Fathers who wished more encouragement and recognition for women would do well to approve a strong declaration of married women's equality. But let the masculine half of the Church be wary of stating that women have "special talents" (even as a tactic in their defense). Everyone should recall that part of the oppression borne by every minority group has been the dominant majority's insistence upon rigid definitions and distinctions. The trouble with limiting categories, whether of praise or blame, is their basic denial of the individual variations of human personality.

If the revolutionary emancipation of women has been slighted by the draft schema, so has yet another revolution within the family: the rising standards of childrearing. New expectations and requirements for childcare exist among most of the world's families, whether they be poor or benefiting from the wealth of urban industrialized nations. There are precious few places in the world where old family patterns of childrearing and education have not been rendered inadequate by the changing conditions of life. The poor family, even in a poor country, may still benefit from the most elementary medical progress. As infant mortality rates drop, parents can expect to raise most of the children they conceive. With new vistas before them, parents will desire not only to keep their children from starvation but to give them adequate diets, medical care, and education. Since all of these good things are expensive, children will no longer contribute to the family economy but consume family resources. For a poor family struggling to survive, each additional child may well endanger the health and welfare of the existing family.

But in affluent families there are also increasing standards for childrearing. In complicated urban societies the children cannot even support themselves without years and years of expensive technical education. In addition to extensive schooling, children in a mobile, fragmented culture will also require more attention, time, and care than in a stable rural society where parents can depend upon traditional structures to convey cultural and religious values, as well as a sense of security. Mobility dispenses with nearby relatives to help in the childrearing or to depend upon in emergencies. Simply to keep a child safe from accidents in an urban mechanized environment requires a constant supervision unheard of in a rural village. New knowledge and new resources and conditions have created a situation in which each child born will need more time, money, and care than the most pampered medieval prince. With higher standards and goals of health, emotional security, religious training, and intellectual stimulation, most affluent parents will not have the psychological and material resources to raise many children well.

In observing modern life, the great new conflict among married people becomes painfully clear and must be recognized by the Church. More children in a family may be detrimental to the common good of the family, yet conceptions will still follow marital intercourse. Indeed, in most countries today, most couples will possess a potential fertility far exceeding the needs of either the individual family or the human race. Man's biological survival upon the planet is more than assured. The problem is now being reversed: too many people threaten the common good of the race. The crisis over birth limitation results from a combination of population pressure and the new conditions of childrearing in urban industrial life. These have created the problem, not an increase of selfish materialism. Earlier in history when war and disease did not curtail population, brutal, inhuman solutions were often practiced, such as starvation of the old, infanticide and widespread abortion. Revolted by such callousness to innocent human life, Christians have always condemned these measures as murder. Other artificial contraceptive measures have also been considered grievously sinful. An absolute relationship between marriage and procreation has been taught. But in the light of modern developments many now question the assumptions of the past.

Upon this controversial and pressing question of birth control the draft schema tried to maintain a delicate balance. While marriage and conjugal love are called valuable themselves for the good of the couple, society, and the Church, the character of conjugal love is described as ordained for the procreation and education of children. The whole concept of the family, the schema continues, arises from the fact that married people are generously disposed to cooperate with the love of their Creator who through them enlarges His own family. Fecundity is a blessing from God and a sign of the fruitfulness of love. Yet it is also recognized that difficulties may at times impose the responsibility of not increasing offspring. The conflict then arising between the good of conjugal love and the need to limit offspring is left as still unresolved by the Church and her ministers who must teach God's law. In conclusion, a plea is made to the faithful to remain undiscouraged and to collaborate with theologians in exploring the serious problem. All are to hope for future practical solutions which will solve these concrete difficulties.

The reaction to this tentative and ambiguous statement was intense and widely divergent. On one hand, attacks came from the conservatives who felt it had gone too far, and, at the other extreme, liberals criticized the statement for not going nearly far enough. The resulting conciliar debates, which still continue throughout the Church, reflect not only widely divergent views about birth control, but reveal the different attitudes and assumptions about marriage and sexuality that govern particular viewpoints. The most conservative attack came from Alfredo Cardinal Ottaviani, Secretary of the Sacred Congregation of the Holy Office, who rejected the suggestion that parents might put limits on the number of children they have. Such freedom, he said, was unheard of in past ages, repudiating the command "to increase and multiply" as well as casting doubt on God's Providence. Cardinal Ottaviani described himself as the eleventh son in a family of twelve whose laboring class parents never doubted God's Providence. Such large families, he maintains, are a more ready source of vocations; all difficulties (excluding health) can be overcome by those imbued with the cross of Christ; it is impossible that the Church erred in its past teaching upon this matter.

Cardinal Ottaviani's conservative protest is that of authentic "folk Catholicism" far removed from the actual teaching of the Church. His objection to the freedom of parents to make prudential judgments about procreation is directly contradictory to the teaching of Pius XII and the established consensus of all theologians. His concept of God's Providence is equally primitive, reminding one of the last defenders of trial by ordeal; if God is the just Ruler of the world, surely He will not let the fire burn an innocent, nor water drown the blameless. A similarly exaggerated reliance upon Providence in procreation may have been justified in past ages when nothing was known of the process of conception. After all, the very knowledge of female ovulation is no older than Cardinal Ottaviani himself. But this discovery together with others of medical science simply changes the boundaries of what can justifiably be left to Providence. When a Jehovah's Witness refuses a blood transfusion for her dying child and calls upon God's Providence, the misguided judgment is obvious. Christ

Himself repudiated the devil's temptation to force an angelic rescue by casting Himself down from the pinnacle of the Temple. Christian parents cannot ignore their knowledge of the procreative process, or their responsibility for the wise use of that knowledge.

As for the argument against birth limitation from the example of an earlier generation, and the dubious connection between large families and vocations, the changing conditions of modern life make these considerations irrelevant. Heroism was easier when there were no alternatives, and when the social conditions were different. Today, each child requires much more preparation before he can earn his livelihood; simple laboring jobs are disappearing. Furthermore, there are no class barriers which would automatically deny education and professional training to the so-called working classes. For that matter, the Church is no longer the only opportunity open for any poor child who shows intellectual talent. Today, the number of vocations in a family is no reliable guide to the holiness and dedication of the parents. More subtle distinctions, a use of interior criteria rather than numerical, must be employed.

The lack of the most elementary distinctions characterized another conservative protest in the Council, that of Ernesto Cardinal Ruffini, Archbishop of Palermo. In objecting to the freedom of married people to judge the number of their offspring, he quoted a scathing passage of St. Augustine. St. Augustine vigorously condemns what "extinguishes within the womb the concealed fetus," "truly a venomous sterility." To Cardinal Ruffini and similar conservative minds, lewdness and lust are as rampant in the modern world as in St. Augustine's day; to give married people freedom to plan families will perforce open the way to abortion—indeed, the difference between contraception and abortion often seems blurred in their minds. If a couple should avoid more offspring, then the use of matrimony is forbidden. One feels here a deep suspicion of rhythm, for Augustine would have surely condemned it as a concession to lust in marriage. Only procreation can justify the use of marriage.

Michael Cardinal Browne, O.P., of the Vatican administrative staff, another conservative critic, also cautioned against urging the right of conjugal love. His contribution to the debate was filled with distinctions, all the traditional distinctions of primary and secondary ends of marriage, natural and unnatural marriage acts, and a new distinction within marital love. In every marriage, according to the cardinal, the spouses have a "love of friendship" for each other and a "love of concupiscence." In the love of friendship the married seek the good of the other, but in the love of concupiscence the spouse seeks only the good of one's self through pleasure of sense. Motivation by the love of concupiscence is distinctly different from marital love of friendship and diminishes it. The implication seems to be that sexual abstinence can purify a marriage from concupiscence.

One trouble with this attitude is that while the distinction between different kinds of love might work perfectly well for friends, it is totally inappropriate for the married. Marriage must go beyond friendship, even to achieve procreation. Married love must include a sensual, sexual friendship, a sexual charity, a drive to physical unity, or, in other words, a "one-fleshness." To give and receive "pleasure of sense" is an important good of marriage, the specifically marital way of expressing the unity of will and heart of traditional friendship. The use of marriage without mutual desire is repugnant and degenerates either into one person using another, or one person coldly withholding a part of himself from the other. The primary aim and discipline of marital love are to achieve a unity of the physical, rational and emotional elements of man's nature. To keep sense pleasure alive and developed is as important (and sometimes as difficult) as to keep a unity of mind and will. It is a misunderstanding of the vocation of marriage to isolate sexuality from the total marriage relationship. This misunderstanding arose from the narrow and mistaken identification of concupiscence with sexual desire. Once it is understood that St. Paul's "flesh" which wars against the Spirit is not simply physical but can include the intellectual and spiritual faculties of men as well, then sexuality's rightful value can be restored.

Such a restoration motivated the liberal side in the Council's debates. For these liberal critics, the schema did not put enough positive emphasis upon married love. Emile Cardinal Léger, Archbishop of Montreal, and Leo Cardinal Suenens, Archbishop of Malines-Brussels, both wished for a stronger assertion of the value of conjugal love apart from procreation. Both called for a fearless renewal of the theology of marriage and a re-examination of the sources of the present teaching to see whether the full implications of Christian marriage have been developed. Melkite-rite Patriarch Maximos IV Saigh added the bold suggestion that the official position of the Church be revised. He condemned both a "bachelor psychosis" and the burden of a Manichaean conception of man that could justify sexuality only in view of the child. He stressed the development of the person and family as a whole over external biological rectitude. In a forceful way, he formulated the question of so many of the faithful: in this present grave crisis of conscience for the immense majority of Christians, can the Council say that God truly wishes this impasse which is so oppressive and against nature? Obviously, the liberals in this great debate wish the Church, either in the schema or in the special papal commission, to review the condemnation of all forms of contraception. Their disagreement with the conservatives is complete.

While granting the persuasiveness of the liberal case one can also sympathize with the conservatives and some of the values they wish to retain. A synthesis is badly needed: a solution which will keep the best of tradition, yet incorporate new insights. To reach this synthesis it should be granted by all that the majority can be wrong, the spirit of the times can be wrong, and development, per se, is not necessarily good. True, the condemnation of usury was gradually revoked, but the early papal protests against the Inquisition were also overridden by the exigencies of the times. Just as disturbing is the thought that for years the majority of the laity would have in conscience endorsed the Arian heresy. Arguments based solely on the needs of the times are unconvincing. The conservatives are right when they insist that a *Christian* solution be sought. The problem of contraceptives cannot be decided in a value vacuum apart from the total Christian message, which does include the Cross. Christians who realize that there is a world to come should face the possibility that Christian demands may be opposed to the reigning solutions of common sense, worldly wisdom, or secular progress. God's ways are not our ways; conceivably, God's laws could contradict all the testimony of all the experts, married laity and the theologians who listen to them. It would be wrong for the Church to countenance contraceptives simply to accommodate consciences which might be in error or to halt defections. Many, many people turned away from Christ when they encountered a hard saying.

But the opposite prior assumptions about the Christian life are also mistaken: difficulties and distress are not intrinsically more Christian than joy and happiness. Whatever is hardest to do is not necessarily God's will. The majority of mankind is not always wrong. Nor is an exaggerated reliance upon the supernatural the most Christian interpretation of Providence. When Christians assert that God created the natural order and at a point in time became man, then they are committed to the goodness of the world so created and so loved. The Catholic witness has always been to a transfiguration of humanity and the world rather than a denial and separation from the total depravity of man and creation. The liberal critics of the traditional teaching about sexuality and marriage are right when they claim that it bears the imprint of Gnostic and Manichaean heresies. The body has been despised. Sexuality has been suspect and considered the chief hindrance to the Spirit. A con-

centration upon the ideals of virginity and its appropriate
mode of life and spirituality has stunted the development of
thinking about the different vocation of marriage.

With a recognition of the false assumptions which can lead
attitudes about marriage astray, theologians can develop a
balanced Christian synthesis. Certainly one corrective needed
is a de-emphasis of the biological, physical elements isolated
from the whole relationship of marriage. Ironically, the emotional rejection of the body seemed to breed a theoretical preoccupation with the physical criteria of intercourse. Perhaps
this was also a result of the reigning judicial, cataloguing,
minimalist mentality, but a Christian attitude must be far different and more demanding. The whole teaching and interpretation of fidelity and marriage rights must be revised. The new
conjugal morality must have new dimensions, demands and
higher standards for the whole personal relationship. Sexual
intercourse should reflect and help create a unity of mind,
heart and desire. When any element is missing, there is serious
imperfection. An isolated desire is recognized as lust, but conjugal acts without love or desire are also degrading to the human person. Such "payments of the debt" are as inadequate as
those monstrous marriages of children once permitted to
solidify family alliances. It is woefully apparent that the
rational judicial mind can create a travesty of a complete ideal
of marriage. Every couple must be enjoined to be "one flesh"
in a living positive way, not simply through consent, contract,
and biological rectitude.

But why should a developed conjugal morality ever permit
artificial interference in the unity of the couple and the procreative processes? Is it necessary that increasing interior
standards of love and a synthesis of body and mind accompany a relaxing of physical standards? At the present time,
abstinence, prolonged or perpetual, is the only permitted form
of family limitation. If a child, the procreative end result of
intercourse, cannot be prudently received without harm to
others already in existence, then the present teaching demands

that the other goods of the conjugal union must also be denied. This demand imposes sexual abstinence upon every married couple whose fertility exceeds their capacities for childrearing. Today, only the sterile, the very rich and extremely healthy are exempted from this sacrifice. The suffering must suffer more.

Prolonged abstinence is difficult both for the immature who have little control of their emotional impulses and for the mature couples who have struggled to obtain a synthesis of mind, desire, and affection. Excluding physical unity from a marriage is rather like stripping the Christian life of the Sacraments. The strong and dedicated can carry on with the non-material channels of communication and love; but even the strong must face an almost inevitable withering and constriction into the self. Yet all of this is still possible for Christians if all of this sacrifice and struggle is truly God's will. Is there no Christian alternative?

Perhaps one method of determining Christian morality is to examine the good one's actions or sacrifices obtain. Abortion and infanticide are horrible crimes because the life of an innocent human person is sacred. (Indeed, as Christians we are given the example of love so great that it lays down its own life for another.) But what is the value preserved by the ban on interfering in the procreative process or conjugal act? Certainly, the integrity of the body and one of its processes is to be respected: wanton mutilation of God's creation, especially the body destined for eternity, is wrong. Yet for sufficient reason all sorts of bodily mutilations have been allowed by the Church. We wince to read that in the past hands could be cut off for punishment of crimes, while applauding the present permission for plastic surgery (for purely psychological benefits) and the transplantation of non-diseased organs from donor to patient. Even a cursory examination of moral theology shows that in every sphere except the sexual the principle of totality, or the good of the person as a whole, transcends the value of physical integrity. Why the exception?

The traditional answers center around the sacred and social nature of sexuality and procreation. It is asserted that since the sexual life-giving powers of man are particularly in God's province, man may not arrogantly usurp God's rights. Or, again, that since the procreative faculty is given to the whole race, and is a substantive good, therefore the sexual process cannot be mutilated for the sake of the individual person or family. Then there is the relatively new argument that the sexual communion of the couple is destroyed when the procreative sign and symbol of their unity are mutilated. While all of these arguments contain some truth, none of them alone or in concert is completely convincing.

The view of the special place of sexuality in God's creation seems an unfounded exaggeration of the hierarchy of Christian values. In the New Testament, words, deeds, attitudes, and even property receive as much or more attention than sexual morality. Sex simply takes its place as an important but not all-important part of human life. Virginity as a counsel of perfection assumes no greater importance than poverty and obedience. Sexual license is certainly castigated, but along with drunkenness, rivalries, and stinginess. Only later did Christians begin to isolate and overemphasize sexual crimes. As rationalism and gnostic influences joined forces, the pleasure, emotional fervor, and physical origin of sexuality made it suspect. Then, too, the lack of knowledge of the procreative processes bred superstition and forced the consignment of sexuality to the realm of mystery. Sexuality became somehow more in God or the Devil's province than property, words, or obedience because so little was known about it all. The ancient pagan and primitive attitude of tabu toward the mysterious became operative. The tabued thing is both feared, despised and overrated for its potent and dangerous attractiveness.

Now that the laws and workings of procreation are known and more is understood of man's psychological make-up, sexuality can be given a balanced and proportionate place in life. A mature Christianity can approach a morality of sexuality without undue fear or superstitious awe. Unfortunately, the secular reaction against sexual repression fostered a sexual mystique which has had its Catholic counterpart. A rapturous romanticism about sex can be as dangerous (and silly) as the past suppressions. Only realism and respect foster the new knowledge which reveals the extent of the responsibilities that God has given man. God instructed man to "fill the earth and subdue it"; subduing the earth will include controlling fertility when controlling death rates has more than filled the world. Man's initiative and control of life are not intrinsically arrogant; such efforts of man can be a grateful cooperation with God who has given the discovery of new knowledge. Indeed, thanksgiving and praise of God can accompany every mastery of nature which furthers the good of persons.

As for the argument that the special social character of sexuality and the good of the race forbid individual mutilation for a greater good, this justification of the Church's condemnation seems dissolved by the changes in our modern world. The human race is no longer threatened by biological extinction. Rather it is the desperate problem of overpopulation that has so quickly come upon the human family. In this complicated situation the common good could well require a widespread forbearance from procreation. The good of the race would only be insured if few children per couple were born. The common good would then require that the exercise of one's procreative powers be an infrequent privilege. Only the most selfish would disregard the needs of the existing community of mankind. Those who argue that procreation is a primary substantive good, imposing upon the married constant procreative obligations, would be hard pressed within their categories and structures formed under totally different human conditions.

The factor which the traditional theorists about procreation ignore or underrate is that of time. Analysis in the abstract takes no account of the sequential events involved in procreation. Perhaps the original biological error of supposing semen to contain miniature men encouraged the confusing of coitus and conception. Would the philosophical linkage of intercourse and procreation have been so complete if the cyclical nature of fertility and sterility had been fully understood? Surely the question of intention is cast in a different light when an individual act of intercourse may not result in conception until three days have passed, not to mention the time span involved in nine months of pregnancy and decades of education and care. The increased life-span of modern women insures that for two-thirds of her life she will be absolutely sterile (not counting the twenty-some sterile days each month during her childbearing years). Within such a context does the artificial achievement of sterility really seem immoral? After all, irreversible sterility comes to every woman at a certain age, precluding the couple's further fertility. To alter the time sequence of human sterility for the good of the person, the family, and the race seems as morally justified as artificially inducing a premature birth for the good of mother and child. Human sterility may affront a primitive pride in procreative prowess, but Christianity has never maintained the pagan measure of a person by the number and vigor of his offspring. The ideal of virginity itself insures the consciousness that while fertility is a blessing of God, there are more important blessings.

There remains, then, the argument (which formerly convinced me) that to mutilate the conjugal act destroys the sign and reality of the couple's loving unity. Since persons are their bodies, their physical actions are not irrelevant. Since, too, the procreative process is the objective given form of unity for physical creativity, so it must be the criteria for the subjective unity and creativity of marital love. Artificial interference with the procreative process of giving and receiving will mutilate the act and the psychological unity. This argument, which is strengthened by man's aesthetic nature, is convincing when applied to perversions, onanism and condoms. When the giving and the receiving of the conjugal act is so basically altered, the mutilation seems total. Interestingly enough, some findings of psychology have confirmed the fact that such total mutilations can have harmful effects upon the human psyche.

But what of the artificial contraceptives which are unobtrusive? Does the knowledge of a sterilizing agent or an unperceived spatial barrier create the same total mutilation? There does seem to be a difference in the degree of imperfection and aesthetic dissatisfaction. In all methods of conception control (including rhythm) the intent is the same; but the integrity of the act is preserved in varying degrees. Naturally, the most perfect conjugal union is one when conception is desired and achieved along with perfect psychological unity. Then all the human potentials of sexuality have been creatively fulfilled. When, however, conception should not take place, unions during the natural periods of sterility preserve the most complete integrity since nothing intrudes upon the couple's psychological unity—if, that is, the couple's sterility is known to be certain. Uncertainty, irregularity, and erratic patterns of sterility can exert such conflicting pressures of anxiety and worry that the psychological unity and mutual sanctification of conjugal love can be destroyed. The stress is created by the conflicts between the obligation of conscience to the imperatives which make conception imprudent and the obligation to the vocation to sexual love and unity—and this stress is compounded by the inability, despite all one's obligations, to be sure of sterility.

In such cases, an artificially induced sterility which is certain does not seem as serious an imperfection as the havoc that anxiety over conception, and conception itself, can bring to the family in its totality. (Of course, if the sterilizing agent is an abortifacient, the situation is totally different.) Indeed, even the unobtrusive mutilation of a conjugal act can seem the lesser imperfection when the total personal and social factors are considered. The integrity of a physical act of unity is a good, since the procreative process is a worthy part of God's creation; but I doubt it is of higher value than a whole person's full development, or a family or society's common good. Sexuality and procreation, like the Sabbath, were made for man, not vice versa. It is better that the basic love, unity, and development of the couple and family be furthered than that physical integrity be maintained whatever the cost. Perhaps soon some new discovery will remove all imperfections by perfecting rhythm; for short periods of abstinence can give to sexuality what silences give to speech. But until the time when knowledge obviates prolonged abstinence and anxiety, the most basic values should be asserted. The Church should refine the traditional teaching and lift the ban on those artificial mechanical methods of birth control that preserve symbolic unity.

This change can be made while still preserving all of the essential values of Christian marriage and family life. Cooperation with God and the sacramental nature of marriage is not vitiated by using certain of the controls that man's God-given rational intellect has invented. Generosity toward God in procreation is only tempered by generosity to the existing family, or the wider human community. Childbearing can become even more of a blessing and a privilege when it is a rare privilege. With control of fertility there is an increasing responsibility and capacity for education of offspring. All of the energy and concern of a family will not be focused upon sheer survival. Individuals within a family can be more generous toward the larger communities of Church and world. Families and marriages which will incorporate high standards of charity and individual development will still be schools of perfection. Naturally, the crosses and sacrifices that accompany all growth toward sanctity will still appear; but there will be no unnecessary sacrifices imposed from without. An exaggerated and isolated misinterpretation of sexuality will add no destructive burdens to the married vocation.

For all these reasons the Church should not hesitate for fear of endangering its authority. Authority exists only to guide the faithful in doing God's will. If the Holy Spirit stirs up doubts about the authority's interpretation of God's will, then let the teachers be willing to change and not cling to the secure habits of tradition. The perfect model and precedent occurred in the first council at Jerusalem with the problem of whether the Gentile converts must be circumcised and observe the Law. Converts from among the Pharisees insisted that the full Law be obeyed. Peter, however, protested at testing God by imposing such a heavy yoke upon the disciples, "a yoke which neither our fathers nor we have been able to bear." After much debate, the Apostles and the Holy Spirit decided to lay upon the new Christians nothing but "the indispensable burden." A few of the symbolically meaningful dietary laws were retained from the panoply of legalistic tabus of eating. These few things which could be easily understood by those who did not know the Law were in substance symbolic spiritual substitutes for the minute distinctions and previous physical requirements for purity.

May Peter's successor today lead the Church into a similar renewal of sexual morality. Let the old yoke of biological laws yield to the liberty of the sons of God. This liberty will bring the new yoke of Christ, but it is an affirmative, all pervasive one involving the internal man and not just external behavior. The Christian focus must be broadened to include the total situation of a married couple and their offspring. With all rationalistic suspicions of the intrinsic evil of the senses allayed, let there be a Christian affirmation that man's sexuality can glorify God though the privilege and blessing of procreation be rare. The married have the special vocation to sanctify their sexual nature through positive affirmation, frequent use and ready responses. The control and asceticism required in this vocation are different from that of the celibate vocation. Since the teachers and the shepherds of the flock almost all follow St. Paul's celibate example, it is important that they recognize with him that "each has his gift from

God." It is most important for the Church to achieve unity of thought when vocations must be different.

To this end, the schema's section on marriage and the family should be more bold and less ambiguous. If the Church cannot teach clearly and affirmatively, then the individual consciences of the faithful should be freed, not confused by pleas to remain obedient yet undiscouraged by insoluble conflicts. Furthermore, the present teaching of the Church should not be alluded to as "God's law" when the problem of just what is God's law is being debated.

Perhaps the papal commission will issue a thorough study that will provide a less ambiguous text. Change through discreet atrophy of anathemas over a century or so may have been possible in the past, but today a conscientious laity and developed communications media make graceful retreat impossible. If Christians have been wrong and have misunderstood or exaggerated some truths to the detriment of others which are now apparent to a developed Christian perception, let us say so and explain in an open and humble way. A concern for secrecy and "saving face" makes only for a craven Christianity—and endless delay. Once the birth control crisis is over, enormous amounts of intellectual and emotional energy can be freed to develop new dimensions of understanding of the dignity of marriage and the family. May the Spirit move the Church most swiftly.

6

The Church
and the World Family

by ADOLPH SCHALK

> Waste and void. Waste and void. And
> darkness on the face of the deep.
> Has the Church failed mankind, or has
> mankind failed the Church?
> When the Church is no longer regarded, not
> even opposed, and men have forgotten
> All gods except Usury, Lust and Power.
>
> T.S. Eliot.*

BACK in 1955 I saw Germany for the first time. In the course of my tour of Bavaria on a motor scooter, I met a young Nigerian medical student. He accompanied me on one of my trips, sitting behind me as we puttered 20 m.p.h. over the picturesque countryside. As we passed village, town, and city, I was quite impressed and even moved by the typical European pattern of the church or cathedral forming the hub or focal point of every community, dominating its physical surroundings—a surviving pattern of the Middle Ages, when the Church was indeed the center of life and it was almost as easy

* From "Choruses from 'The Rock' in *Collected Poems 1909–1962*" by T.S. Eliot. Reprinted by permission of Harcourt, Brace & World, Inc.

to be a Catholic as it was to breathe. "Europe is the Faith and the Faith is Europe," the famous Bellocian phrase came often to mind.

Not so my agnostic friend, a "fallen-away" Catholic. At home in Nigeria he had already begun the process of faith-losing, as he claimed, because of the contradiction that everywhere confronted him, that of Catholics and Protestants of many sects, competing and bickering with each other, each claiming to be Christianity, each belittling the other.

In Germany, his gradual awareness of the monstrosity of the Hitler era and the collaboration (through involvement and support every bit as well as through appalling lack of commitment) of the Churches, Catholic and Protestant alike, completed the damage.

"How," he said sadly, reacting quite differently to the sight of so many church steeples, "could a country with so many churches start a war?"

Then, a couple of years ago, I toured Yugoslavia. I couldn't help but be stirred by the impressive sight of Zagreb's magnificent cathedral, whose steeples are said to be the highest in the world. But visitors to the penthouse night club of the nearby skyscraper, which towers higher than the magnificent steeples, can look down on the cathedral, and I am sure many do so in more ways than one. In another city the values that men live by in that country are embodied in the name "Tito, Tito, Tito, Tito" shining in neon from all four sides of a skyscraper, while elsewhere the name of this benevolent big brother glows electrically from a mountainside.

During a trip to Poland recently I found the churches everywhere overflowing and learned that an estimated twenty-seven million persons, or 95 per cent of the population, are practicing Catholics. Here some five thousand pilgrims annually march on foot, seventeen miles per day, the 140 miles from Warsaw to Czestochowa, sleeping en route not in comfortable hotels (there are none anyway), but literally on the roadside, in the fields and barns.

I, by contrast, was sped comfortably by express train in the direction of the famous shrine. There, as I walked from the terminal to the monastery of Jasna Gora (Shining Mountain), I was soon joined by throngs of singing, praying pilgrims, some of them towing life-size crosses or crucifixes. There were countless hundreds of shawled peasant women, carrying their provisions in checkered handkerchiefs, and deeply tanned, leather-skinned men, looking like extras in a Tolstoy movie, pouring in from the trains, roads, and side streets into a river of humanity. Dozens of mud-spattered horsedrawn covered wagons carried the sick, the aged, and children.

In season and out of season they come, every day of the year, by the thousands and thousands from every corner of Poland to pray at the shrine of the "Black Madonna," the famed painting that is so named because it was darkened by fire and which has escaped plundering, siege and war over the centuries, and which legend says is the work of St. Luke himself. On the Feast of the Assumption, August 15, the crowd swells to over a hundred thousand and gathers on the vast field below the monastery wall, where, in the presence of Stefan Cardinal Wyszynski, the Primate of Poland, they renew their annual vows to keep the country Catholic.

But veteran observers are beginning to question the longevity of this kind of religious exuberance, geared as it is to the peasant mentality and much of which, if the truth be told, is hard to distinguish from superstition. Cardinal Wyszynski, together with most of the Polish hierarchy, have been strongly criticized, not only by the Communists but also by loyal priests and laymen of the Church, for a too rigid and inflexible stand against the regime. Worst of all, the critics charge, this attitude has made the Church authorities generally passive toward Council reforms. Precious little is being done, they say, to prepare for the profound changes that are bound to affect the Church as a vastly peasant population rapidly becomes sophisticated by the breakneck speed of modernization. In the cities one already notices a growing number of youth, and even of middle-aged, who are drifting away from the Church, which no longer appears to mean anything to them.

"Ironically," one priest told me, "one of the greatest threats to the Church in Poland today is the West. The impact of jazz, modern clothes, a higher standard of living, together with an almost frenzied interest in everything American, has come too quickly. To be quite frank, I must confess that I am more afraid of losing the youth through secularism than communism."

One hesitates to reach hasty conclusions, but if the present trends continue, Poland may well be hurtling down the same road on which another country—one which still inaccurately has the prefix "Catholic" attached, namely Austria—is already traveling. For here the estrangement of the Church from modern life is already an established fact.

A cursory glance at the book, *Die Katholiken in Österreich*, a sociological study by Erich Bodzenta, reveals just a few of the staggering challenges of the Church in Austria.

Although the country is nominally 95 per cent Catholic (one is never more than a ten-minute walk from a church in Vienna), the study shows that Austria, for all her Advent wreaths, *"Grüss Gott,"* wayside shrines, and inns with such religious names as *"Augegottes"* (the Eye of God), can hardly qualify as a Catholic country any more. Bodzenta discloses that by actual survey approximately 70 per cent of all parishes in Austria can be characterized as lukewarm and indifferent.

A positive development can be seen in the decline of divorces (eleven out of a thousand marriages in 1948 as against five out of a thousand in 1959). On the other hand, persons married three or four times are no longer an oddity in Vienna. And conspicuously absent from the study is mention of the high incidence of abortion (some secular sources, including the Bavarian statistical office, cite figures that place Austria among the countries with the highest abortion rates).

The study further reveals that, on the basis of a scientific poll, in the Archdiocese of Vienna, with 1,373,713 baptized

Catholics registered, only 226,476 or 19.5 per cent regularly attend Sunday Mass. Of those who do attend Sunday Mass, one-third attend churches other than their own parishes. The number of persons leaving the Church in Austria has increased considerably since 1945. During the first postwar years twice as many left as in 1945, then four times as many; by 1952 twelve times as many. Since then the dropout rate has declined to "only" six times that of 1945.

In Holland, according to the *Katholiek Sociaal Kerkelijk Institut*, only 25 per cent of Catholics in urban areas go to Sunday Mass regularly.

Over in England, W. N. T. Roberts, writing in *The Tablet* (May 9, 1964), discusses the declining church attendance. On the basis of parish priests' estimates reported annually to their bishops, total attendance at Sunday Mass averaged over a number of Sundays, is only about 2,100,000 or less than 40 per cent.

I don't have any study of Italy available, but the mere mention of one single item makes me shudder to think what a full-fledged study, if any exists, would reveal: Rome, the religious heart of Catholicism, repeat, the Diocese of *Rome*, had, in 1964, an ordination class of—*one*.

The list could be multiplied *ad nauseam*, but the entries would all boil down to the same thing: that in the once Christian strongholds the Church is discredited; that Belloc's famous dictum, viewed in the light of today's situation, is so much nostalgic nonsense; that so far as the family of nations is concerned, the Church is fighting with her back to the wall.

I really don't think American Catholics realize just how far gone the Church is in many parts of the world, especially Europe. For back home the illusion of expansion is continually nursed by our comfortable middle-class Catholicism with our plushly carpeted rectories, Xerox machines and IBM punchcard apparatuses and all the rest of the business paraphernalia that in itself could become a far more dangerous threat to the spirit of the Church than external enemies. The illusion of expansion is further enhanced by the impressive numbers of daily communicants and the throngs packing our churches every Sunday.

Heartening, however, is the magnificent, refreshing, child-like and often quite dynamic Catholicism spreading throughout parts of Asia and Africa, of a kind that vies with the simplicity of the early Christians. But these advances, thrilling as they are, are illusory when viewed from a global perspective.

For the plain, sobering fact is that the population growth of humanity is increasing far more rapidly than membership in the Church or, for that matter, the entire conglomerate of the Christian Churches. The resurgence of Buddhism and Islam already shows signs of outstripping Christian gains in Africa and Asia, while the Christian Churches, alas, are all too slowly shedding their ignominious association with colonialism.

According to the French demographer Adrian Bouffard, only 20 per cent of the world's population will still be Christian by the year 2,000, as compared with 35 per cent in 1900. The Church, in other words, is a diminishing minority.

It is more than a mere physical discrepancy between the world and the Church that one sees from the upper stories of the R.C.A. Building in Manhattan, from which St. Patrick's Cathedral looks like a toy (and the association of the Church with something to do with children is not exactly far-fetched in the minds of many people). The Cologne Cathedral is still an impressive sight, dominating as it does the skyline of that city, but the reality that men live by is far more aptly expressed by the symbol one sees on the Autobahn a few miles away, the gigantic electric Bayer sign (the name in the form of a cross). In Copenhagen the hub of the city is the SAS skyscraper. Over in Dublin the day may well begin with Mass, but as a full-page ad in *Time* (European edition) put it, "dawn over Dublin" really begins with a certain electrical firm whose bulbs "light up the city," whose dictating machines, food mixers, hair dryers, television and radio sets "enrich life from Cork to Killarney," and at night the Irish end the day with the firm's electric blanket. (Grace, a priest in a catechism class long ago explained, can be compared to electricity.)

"The destinies of the world" are guided by men who wear a certain kind of watch, and if Christ asked all to come to Him who seek to be refreshed, everybody knows where to find the real pause that refreshes. The time is not too far off when men who know values best will realize that Halo Soap is the "soap that sanctifies," and that you can check your breath before your next confession with "Garglies," the throat purifier.

How do you fight a thing like this? There used to be a time when the Church had enemies. Today the great tragedy is that the Church has no enemies—except the intangible enemy of being ignored. She is no longer taken seriously enough to be attacked. Nothing has become more meaningless than apologetics and the once proud challenge of defending the Church. The problem now is showing that she has any relevance at all.

The Church's estrangement from the family of man is all the more aggravated by the world-wide upheaval of cultures. The sweep of modernization in the developing countries, the vast migration of millions, not only within the various countries but from country to country and from continent to continent, amounts to a universal creeping erosion of cultural and national (as opposed to nationalistic) values and traditions. To an unprecedented degree men are losing their identities. This may have the beneficial by-product of helping to do away with nationalism, but at the same time it is sweeping away the ties that bind men to ideologies and values, good and bad, but values nonetheless, without which life is empty and meaningless.

I happen to live in Switzerland, a small country that could easily fit inside Lake Michigan with room to spare. Its current native population is just over five million. In spite of many deficiencies, the country holds up to the world, in the words of Walter Lippmann, "a shining example of democracy," containing as it does people of four completely different languages and cultures (German, French, Italian and Romansch), who live harmoniously together.

Today this harmony is being threatened by the tremendous social problems caused by the presence of nearly a million foreigners living within its borders. Though the Swiss have themselves to blame for much of the foreign immigration (Italians by the tens of thousands do much of the menial work few Swiss want to do), the current wave of xenophobia proceeds from a very real—and understandable—concern about losing their own character. "I feel," one Swiss put it to me, "like a stranger in my own country."

But Switzerland is not alone. The United Kingdom is facing a very similar crisis as countless thousands of persons from every Commonwealth country in the world, of all races and nationalities, pour into the British Isles. In West Germany there are so many foreigners (1.3 million at last count) that in a recent opinion poll the majority of the respondents expressed their willingness to work an hour a week longer if this would help slow down the pace of immigration. A few examples will suffice to illustrate the effect of such foreign saturation. When I recently drove straight through West Germany, from Hamburg to Zurich in a leisurely two-day trip, my fluent German was often useless to me because so many of the waiters and hotel attendants spoke only Greek, Italian, Spanish, or even Turkish. There is such a labor shortage in the Federal Republic that the West German railroads have reached all the way to North Africa to find employees and even went to the expense of altering whole sections of railroad coaches and embellished them with prayer rugs, so that the Moslem workers could bow to Mecca at the appropriate times. It is an open secret that Swiss cuckoo clocks are actually made in the Black Forest region of Germany because wages there are lower, and certain Swedish products are manufactured in Spain for the same reason.

Moreover, there is every indication that this mass human migration, whether caused by immigration, business, politics, or just plain tourism, will not only continue but will escalate to immense proportions as world-wide improvements in living standards increase the travel potential. In Western Europe alone, some sixty million persons spent vacations outside of their own countries in 1963.

Of course not all nations will change with equal rapidity, and chances are that some nations may preserve their traditions for several generations. The new emerging nations in Africa especially will be preoccupied with their national character for a long time to come. But these national trends are only temporary, and over a longer period the customs even in those nations will predictably succumb to the onrush of modernization.

This gradual corrosion of national traditions and values could be a tremendous blessing if it were replaced by a global set of values, a new emergence of mankind as a great human family. But there is a grave danger that something entirely different could evolve. For already the traditions (more and more kept alive only at government expense for the benefit of tourists) are dying out and being replaced by a frightening odorless, colorless, plastic world of uniformity, a world where everybody eats from the same synthetic plates from Tokio to Wichita and laughs at the same comic strips (Jiggs and Maggie can even be found in Belgrade's *Borba*, and they "speak" in the same Cyrillic letters as used in the Russian language), and listens to the same Beatles. And here is the paradox. We are engulfed in a world of increasing uniformity, while at the same time the world is becoming an ever greater babble of disunity.

It is precisely here where the Church faces the greatest challenge in her history. She has been characterized since the Middle Ages primarily by Western, European structures, institutions, mentality. Today this identification has been seriously called into question and the Church is called upon at last to face up to her global responsibilities.

This shift of focus became especially clear to me during a

very illuminating interview I enjoyed during the Third Session of the Council with Archbishop Denis E. Hurley, O.M.I., of Durban, South Africa. A tall, youthful-looking man, with rugged but handsome features and a crisp, quiet way of talking, he spoke frankly and to the point. When I asked him for his chief over-all impression of the Council, he replied: "For me it's the end of an epoch of the Church that goes back centuries. I think we're winding up what has come to be referred to as the Constantinian epoch. This goes back to Constantine. That makes it 1,600 years old. It has been characterized, I would say, by the close association of the Catholic Church with Western Latin culture, the culture that grew out of Western Europe. So much so that in the Middle Ages they couldn't tell where Church ended and State began. What were the temporal duties of a pope and what were the spiritual obligations of an emperor? Everything was pretty confused. And that has gone on in some of its applications right up to our time. Now I think this Council is writing the concluding chapter of that epoch just in time to prepare the Church, to freshen up the Church, to rejuvenate the Church, to purify the Church, to clarify her goals, so that she can move into what appears to be a new epoch in the life of humanity.

"I think we're just in time and that very, very exciting years lie ahead of us. I find it hard to find a Council of the Church in the past that compares with it in terms of importance. Perhaps the Council of Jerusalem, which wasn't an ecumenical council but was the gathering of the apostles and presbyters to decide whether or not to depart from Jewish custom and Jewish law. That was an epoch-making decision at the time. It freed the Church for all of her subsequent work. And what we're doing now is to free the Church from medieval and post-medieval culture, with all respect, of course, for the achievements of the past and making use of what we can still use, but nonetheless to free the Church from that and liberate her, purify her, strengthen her, and to go forward into the future—to illuminate and to consecrate a new culture. But I think we'll never make the same mistake of getting so linked with that culture, the mistake we made in the past."

Archbishop Hurley, it seems to me, here puts the finger on the heart of the problem concerning the Church and the family of nations. In the past, the very link with Western culture was the Church's crowning glory and, as far as Europe was concerned, it was the latter's principle of unity. "It was," writes Christopher Dawson in *Understanding Europe*, "in religion that Europe found its original basis of unity. . . . It was as Christendom that Europe first became conscious of itself as a society of peoples with common moral values and common spiritual aims."

In time, however, this very principle of unity became a principle of uniformity, and the Church has suffered greatly throughout the world because of the tendency to impose, not the faith that united Europe, but the European culture that the faith united, in the mission field.

Today Europe is groping for a new unity and many observers deplore the fact that the emphasis is economic and, from a long-range viewpoint, political, but without the Church. The Common Market in Brussels, the European Parliament in Strasbourg, Euratom and EFTA, along with the European Coal and Steel Community, are bringing ever closer the possibility of a political union of Europe; but with the Church playing a quite insignificant role as a unifying factor. This may be all to the good. The disintegration of the old European values, for which the Church was largely responsible, deplorable as this is, has, however, at the same time loosened the Church from her strictly Western moorings and set her adrift to the world. She who was once the principle of unity for a thing called *Abendlaendische Kultur* (Western culture and civilization) is now challenged to become the principle of unity for the world family of nations.

Paradoxically enough, it is the new opening toward diversity that will help, rather than hinder, the Church to become this principle of unity. In a world family of nations threatening to lose their values and traditions, the Church could become the great preserver of these treasures because she transcends them. And she transcends them precisely to the extent that she can also identify herself in all nonessentials with local and regional cultural expressions. The introduction of the vernacular, the greater appreciation of the various rites, including the colorful Ethiopian Rite, and the use of tom-toms, and even certain dances during Mass are expressions of this new diversity. National cultures and traditional customs will less readily degenerate into nationalistic expressions if they are inspired by a transcendental unity.

This unity amid diversity could prove to be a powerful antidote to the frightening collectivization in industry, in daily life and in government that threatens the world from the West every bit as much as from the East. Some scholars even see Western trends toward collectivization as more dangerous because they are so imperceptible and apparently without ideology. Nothing nourishes uniformity so much as a lack of a principle of unity; conversely, nothing encourages diversity so much as unity at the core.

Seen in this light, the prospect of a numerically dwindling Christianity need not frighten us. It is only when the problem is approached on a mathematical basis that the solution seems hopeless. Nothing is more futile in the over-all picture as the numbers game and the illusory reliance on individual conversions, desirable as this is in some areas. Rather, the task that seems to confront the Church is that of creating the kind of climate in which her unchanging values can be made comprehensible and relevant to a colorful and diverse world. The time is past when men can be persuaded to join the Church as a kind of a spiritual insurance company; rather the Church should so serve men that they of themselves no longer wish to do without her.

When during the Third Session the Council took up Schema 13, "The Church in the Modern World," the discus-

sion seemed doomed from the start. Characterized as it was by
vague generalities, it could have degenerated into a disappointing panacea, solving no problems because it tried to solve all
of them. How could the Church at one and the same time offer
directives to people and still avoid pat, know-it-all answers?
Particularly in regard to the family of nations, how could one
document do justice to the galaxy of problems besetting
Americans, Europeans, Asians, Latin Americans, Africans?
Clearly any attempt at actual solutions could only embarrass
the Church before the world.

As Bishop John J. Wright of Pittsburgh put it in his remarks introducing chapter 4 of the schema: "It is not . . .
our intent to develop individual points in detail nor attempt
easy and over-ready answers which could only be glib and in
the long run deceptive. Nor is it our intent to undertake the
exploration of all the 'signs of the times' one by one. This
would be the work of many years. . . .

"This chapter should not be the *final* word of the Council's
dialogue with the world, but the *first*. Indeed, on our side, it
should be but the beginning of the presentation of the case
for the teachings of the Church. It represents our desire to
open new doors to new contacts in order to accomplish immediately some first objective, to set up guidelines for the
dialogue, to dispose of certain prejudices and to set up protec-
tions against false tendencies."

In short, the schema did not and could not offer clear-cut
answers to the modern world, but it does provide the basis for
a magnificent proclamation of an attitude. Thus, while a
panacea approach to the world's ills is neither desirable nor
possible, a change in some of the basic attitudes and their consistent and sustained implementation in specific structural areas
is entirely realistic.

So far as the family of nations is concerned, it seems to me
that first and foremost the Church must become more of a
family herself. Nothing is more alien to the modern world and
nothing will frustrate the Church's efforts at *aggiornamento*

more than a rigid adherence to her feudal structure. The court atmosphere, the throne, crown and scepter symbolism should all be seriously examined.

One should not, of course, lightly dismiss traditions and customs that preserve continuity with the past. As Bishop Wright once said to me in a private interview: "I believe that man lives by symbols, that's why women wear wedding rings. The hearts of the best men thrill at symbols. Think of the presidential seal. We are instinctively liturgical, laughing ceremonial animals." Commenting on Swiss guards he added, "someone has to handle the crowds. . . . Good taste should be the criterion."

A step in the right direction has already been made by Pope Paul VI. He has abolished the most lavish of cardinals' garments and their three-yard-long cloaks "as a sign of humility and poverty on the part of cardinals."

There was widespread speculation before the 1965 consistory that Pope Paul had considered letting the College of Cardinals die a natural death, by relegating them to a secondary position and substituting a new senate of bishops, an idea promoted by the Council, which would be located in Rome or at least convene frequently there, and which would have jurisdiction over the Curia. For reasons best known to himself, the Holy Father met the proposal with a compromise, at least for the present.

There is some consolation in the fact that the college has indeed expanded to an international group, with far greater non-Italian representation than heretofore. But one might ask whether such partial solutions might not easily slip into habit and thus postpone indefinitely any hope of replacing the college with a senate.

Along with this, of course, is the urgent need for a complete overhaul of the Roman Curia, structurally and staff-wise, and its total internationalization, with built-in permanent guarantees that it remain so, and its permanent decentralization through the establishment of national bishops' conferences.

While no responsible Catholic would wish for a non-Italian pope just for the sake of having a pope of another nationality, it is hoped that future popes should not be automatically eliminated solely because they are non-Italian. A de-Italianizing of the entire Vatican structure is a *sine qua non* for truly internationalizing the Church and one of the best ways of speeding up this process is to make it possible *de facto* and not just *de jure* to have a non-Italian pope.

Psychological blocks standing in the way of reform can be overcome by removing, or at least decreasing, the regal symbols and aristocratic trappings of the Church which are so repugnant to many emerging peoples. After all, these royalist trappings are a relatively recent accretion and a departure from the more pronounced familial symbols that characterized the more biblically-orientated Church of the early centuries. To be sure, the early Church was not entirely free from royalist influences and Christ Himself sometimes used the kingly symbol in His parables. But surely His own behavior—one thinks of his visits with Mary and Martha, of the Last Supper, and of *His* dialogue with the world—of all these were pre-eminently those of a Father and brother rather than a king. His kingdom was never meant to be one of this world. (I shall leave to theologians the thorny problem of how to interpret "The King of the Jews" and the feasibility of considering the abolishment of the feast of Christ the King in favor of a more familial one.)

We speak of the Holy *Father* and we call our priests "Father" (though this is more of an English-speaking form of address and it is not at all common to many other countries of the world). But is it not difficult to think of the Pope as a Father when he comes riding into St. Peter's on a portable throne, symbolizing the regal authority and pomp of command instead of the paternal authority of love?

During the third session of the Council, which was among other things a genuine breakthrough for women, the thought suddenly occurred to me that the role of men (as *men*, not as laymen) has hardly been discussed at all, either in the Council or elsewhere. From Grailville to *Commonweal* the focus has been on women. One looks in vain for a book or article on the lost concept of the father in our society. Our Father may indeed be in His heaven, but from the importance attached to Him one would hardly know it.

Yet never in human history has there been a greater need for a genuine restoration of the father to his rightful place in the family, in the nation, in the world family of nations, and especially in the Church. Is it far-fetched to see a relation between this lack of fatherhood—and the responsibilities and glory attached thereto—and the alarming increase of homosexuality throughout the world, especially in urban centers, and the explosion of children who grow up without their fathers? One certainly welcomes the long overdue emancipation of women in every area, and especially in the Church, but at the same time one wonders what is happening to the male of the species who has degenerated to a large degree to an emasculated, apron-wearing, henpecked and irresponsible milquetoast.

I may be wrong, but I suspect that, precisely because women are downgraded in the Church, an undue amount of feminine emphasis has crept into our services, has sugarized our art, has turned our vestments and altar boys' attire into insulting display window dressing, and has emasculated our music. I submit that it was the very absence of women from influence in the Church that has encouraged this sickening effeminate influence. And I venture to predict that, by giving them a rightful place in the Church, both clericalism and momism would considerably decline, because then the need for a celibate clergy for continual compensation would disappear.

At any rate, the Church can only assume its role as a family in the world family of nations if it "girds up its loins like a man," if it restores to its pre-eminent place the lost Fatherhood of God, and if it replaces the dead symbols of royalty and aristocracy with the dynamic symbols of a living family.

If the Church is to be a family, and if it is willing to shed its obsolete feudalist trappings, then another important step, it seems to me, is to do away with the fiction of the Vatican as a sovereign country and turn it into a bona fide international center of faith.

An intelligent, fairminded nonbeliever, say an American, making a tour of Europe, might be fascinated by the handful of vest-pocket kingdoms like Monaco, Liechtenstein, Andorra and San Marino. Going on to see the Vatican, as far as he can make out with his only too human eyes, it differs little from the others, whose chief industries are postage stamps, picture postcards and tourism. Leaving aside St. Peter's and the truly great works of art and architecture, which one would not for the world wish to abolish or belittle, much of the remaining atmosphere embarrassingly resembles a musical comedy. How can a nonbeliever take a Church, so closely identified with operetta props and jargon, seriously? Nothing is more ludicrous than to see the Vatican's Swiss and other guards dust off their rusty tin horns and motheaten uniforms for a state visit. Like a handful of lady bugs on a grey suit, they are just a few specks in the vastness of St. Peter's square, while their tinny music is drowned out by the traffic grinding past. "What," the bewildered agnostic visitor may well ask, "has all this got to do with loving my neighbor and saving my soul?"

"The State of Vatican City," writes Irving Levine, in his trenchant book, *Main Street, Italy*, "is a most singular community. Guidebooks are fond of describing the Vatican as the world's smallest independent state. Small it is, but its independence is more romantic than realistic. In actual fact, it is an artificial state without many attributes of a genuine and sovereign nation."

If this is the case, is it not time that serious thought were given to the possibility of giving up this momentous fiction?

If we are going to have an open Church, it seems that the first step would be to have an open Vatican. And if we are going to have a truly international Church, it seems logical that the Vatican must also become truly international.

Just a cursory glance at some of the Vatican's procedures and structure reveal that at present the contrary is the case. What should be an international center of faith open to all is a tightly guarded enclave, admission to which is complicated, time-consuming, inefficiently and often arbitrarily dispensed. Then there is the matter of the Church's finances. One has to turn to secular publications (*Time* and the German counterparts of *Time* and *Life, Der Spiegel* and *Der Stern*) to learn that the Vatican's wealth is estimated at between $10 billion and $15 billion, that the Vatican owns shares, in some cases controlling shares, in the Bank of Rome (*Banco di Roma*), in the Commercial Bank (*Banca Commerciale*) and a bank with the intriguing name—but of highly questionable taste—Bank of the Holy Ghost (*Banco di Santo Spirito*). This latter is an extension of the papal treasury during the seventeenth century, when the pope held large territories. The Vatican also owns, according to *Der Spiegel* (May 27, 1964), controlling stock of most public utilities in Italy (gas, electricity, water, telephone, transportation), while its gold reserves are on deposit with the Federal Reserve Bank of New York. And the sole owner of Vatican City is the pope.

No parliament, no board of directors, no stockholders, no cabinet of ministers, no electorate, but the pope and his aides alone administer these vast funds. No other institution in the world enjoys anything near this kind of freedom of action and total unaccountability to anyone.

Certainly the Church needs vast funds to carry out its far-flung commitments around the world and no one can seriously question that it is spending this money for worthy purposes. But we have arrived at a time when the Church is trying to stop asking always what is in the best interests of herself as an institution and is starting to ask what is in the best interests of humanity. Accordingly, it is not improper to ask: Is humanity best served by the Church when its vast resources are concentrated in the hands of one single human being whose infallibility is restricted to matters of faith and morals and even then within the narrow confines of *ex cathedra* pronouncements?

Fortunately we have been blessed in recent generations with good, sometimes holy, men in the office of the papacy, whose lives have been models of frugality and simplicity. But who is to say it is entirely beyond the realm of possibility that another Alexander VI, or a far more subtle representative of abuse, could one day ascend to the papacy? Or, for that matter, what is to prevent a mentally or physically afflicted—or just plain foolish—pope from causing universal havoc through his misuse of these enormous funds? At the very core of the Church there are no provisions that could protect the Church and the humanity it serves from such an unlikely but nevertheless always possible prospect.

There is little likelihood that the pope would relinquish his temporal responsibilities, and perhaps there are equally strong reasons for his keeping them as there might be for such abandonment. Nevertheless, the secrecy which surrounds the Vatican and its fiscal activities does not make it any easier for the world to believe that these monies are always used wisely and well. By openly showing a detailed published budget regularly to the world the Vatican could help dispel a great deal of cynicism among countless thousands of otherwise good-willed persons. More important, by placing the entire sum of Vatican assets into the hands of an international body of experts, heavily represented by laymen, under the controlling direction of—please God—a senate of bishops, the world could see also that differences of opinion are given a hearing before these sums are allocated for specific purposes. Above all, Catholics and non-Catholics alike would be continually reassured that the Church has nothing to hide and that its interests are in fact identical with those of humanity itself.

The Church is supposed to be not only Catholic but also catholic. Yet the Vatican has a long way to go before it is truly international. Aside from the use of a number of lan-

guages and the presence within Vatican City of a German
cemetery and an Ethiopian college with twenty-three students, the place is dominated by the Italians—in administration,
in culture, in language, in exasperating business methods, in
mentality. No one for a moment wishes to belittle this great
ethnic group of the world, and if anything the present writer
is partial to these people whom he loves dearly. But if the
Church is truly to be partial to the human family first of all,
then there is no other choice but to open up those Vatican
gates at last and let in the human race!

The Vatican Museum has one of the greatest and most magnificent collections of art in the world, but one looks in vain
for a single item produced in the twentieth century, nor does
that institution begin to balance its predominantly European
works of art with works from Africa, Asia, Australia and the
Americas.

The Vatican Library boasts some 700,000 volumes, including ancient unbound manuscripts and some in Egyptian
papyri. It is characterized by such thoroughness that a re-
searcher, requesting an ancient tome listed in the catalogue,
received a slip with the notation, "missing since 1530." What
is really needed, however, is a slip referring to books of our
time with the notation, "present, as of now." The Library
does not come near to being as international as the Library of
Congress, or, for that matter, even the Lenin Library in
Moscow.

Nothing is less international than the *Osservatore Romano*, printed as it is in Italian and orientated to the previous
century.

If the atmosphere in Vatican City resembles that of a cemetery, nothing conveys this atmosphere to the world more
accurately than Radio Vatican. It sits on one of the hottest
news beats of the world, but foreign correspondents attempting to monitor the station for leads and background information soon give up in frustration.

To really find out what is going on at the Vatican one must

turn to the great secular news media of the world: BBC, *The New York Times* and *New York Herald Tribune, Time* and *Newsweek,* a handful of penetrating Catholic journals, such as *The Commonweal, The National Catholic Reporter,* and the *Catholic Herald* of London, and such highly successful TV documentaries as those shown in Sweden and produced in Rome by Gunnar D. Kumlien. One of the pleasant ironies of the Council is that it should get such a magnificent press coverage, not because of, but in spite of adequate Vatican cooperation. Considering the enormous obstacles that stand in the way of Vatican news coverage, it is quite an achievement that the Vatican gets as much favorable treatment as it does.

All this points to the great need for the establishment of an international Catholic information and communication center, with full-time lay press officers on hand to serve the world press and perhaps even a separate section for the public. Devoutly to be wished would be the reorganization of Vatican Radio into a bona fide international radio station under the direction of qualified lay experts with full liberty to produce stimulating documentaries and features equal to the standards, say, of the BBC. It would not exactly be a bad idea either completely to revamp the *Osservatore Romano* into an international Catholic observer, also under the direction of an international staff of lay journalists in tune with the modern world, with editions in, at the very least, the several major languages of the world, English, French and Spanish (or German) and Russian and Chinese. Official announcements could be made in a special section, while the rest of the newspaper could assiduously balance liberal with conservative viewpoints on all subjects. What is needed is a comprehensive, world-orientated newspaper, technically and editorially equal at least to the *Christian Science Monitor.* Then the task of reading the Church's semi-official newspaper would not be a tedious duty of a select group of newsmen, theologians and diplomats, but a pleasant occupation. More important, a highly useful service would be rendered by the Church to the world, especially since most of the laity still have little awareness of what is going on in the Church, in spite of the Council and in spite of the billions of words written about it.

Back in January of 1962, the famous Father Riccardo Lombardi, S.J., founder of the Movement for a Better World, recommended in his controversial book, *The Council*, a world senate of laymen, which would make sweeping changes in the Church's administrative procedures. Nothing much has been heard of this idea, or, for that matter, Father Lombardi, since then, but it might well be worthy of study. Along this same vein, Miss Catherine Buehler, one of the leading delegates at the First Congress of the Lay Apostolate in Rome in 1951, during an interview at the Council proposed a Council of the Laity. Such a lay council, she said, would have particular relevance to the schema on the Church in the modern world. A lay council, she added, could be attended by experts in every field, from mass communications, social work, science, technology, to family relations and the lay apostolate.

Moreover, such a council might well point the way to the heart of the solution of the problem of relevance. If the Church has thus far failed to get through to people, perhaps it is because the chief instrument for such communication, the layman, has been neglected. By giving more responsibility, all the way up to the top echelons of the Church, to laymen, the Church will automatically find the way to relevance, because it is, after all, laymen who are compelled day in and day out to come to grips with the world. They, too, have the know-how in every conceivable field to implement the vague generalities voiced by the Council Fathers. Such a lay council would provide the broad outlines of the Council Fathers with realistic possibilities for implementation.

The text of Schema 13 glowingly states the Church's concern for economic development, for helping the developing nations, for generous international collaboration in the solution of the demographic problem, for full participation with international organizations. But never in a million Council years will the Church achieve these aims until and unless it has developed the structures and techniques to implement them.

It is no longer enough for the Church to be, through the Vatican, a member of UNESCO (the United Nations Educational, Scientific, and Cultural Organization), or of FAO (the UN's Food and Agricultural Organization), or the UN's International Agency for Atomic Energy. The real need is for a permanent agency of laymen devoted to implementation.

It is thrilling to hear of Joseph Cardinal Ritter's wonderful priest corps, and the plans of the St. Louis archbishop to send ten per cent of the St. Louis diocesan clergy to serve in Latin America by 1975. This is certainly an example to be emulated, and is a new shift of the Church toward its global responsibilities. But such a move, wonderful in itself, is not sufficient in the over-all problem of making the Church relevant among the family of nations.

A hint in the direction of the true solution, it seems to me, was made by the magnificent speech on the Council floor during Session Three by a layman, James J. Norris, of Rumson, New Jersey, who is president of the International Catholic Migration Commission and also assistant to the executive director of the National Catholic Welfare Conference—Catholic Relief Services.

Speaking in fluent Latin, Norris called the world a "lopsided community" in which one small group of North Atlantic nations own 70 per cent of the world's wealth, although they represent only 16 per cent of the world's peoples. "Meanwhile," he added, "three-quarters of the human race live in the state of poverty bordering on or below the subsistence level."

The solution to this problem, Norris said, was "*in aid, in trade, and in the transfer of skills.*" Then he went on to appeal to the Ecumenical Council to issue "a clarion call for action which would involve *the creation of a structure that would devise the kind of institutions, contacts, forms of cooperation and policy which the Church can adopt,* to secure full Catholic participation in the world-wide attack on poverty." (Italics mine.)

Here is the heart of the matter. The layman *already* possesses the relevant contact with the world. Once he is given the authority and the structural vehicle to work in the name of the Church, the problem of relevance, the problem of getting through to the world and the family of nations, will solve itself.

T. S. Eliot's question, then, as to who failed whom, remains a largely rhetorical one. The question's challenge, however, is not hard to find. Dietrich Bonhoeffer, the Evangelical theologian who died in a Nazi concentration camp, wrote from his prison cell, *"Der Mensch ist nicht für die Kirche da, sondern die Kirche ist für den Mensch da"* (Man is not here for the Church, but the Church is here for man). That is to say, *"Man ist nicht Mensch um Christ zu sein, sondern man is Christ um Mensch zu sein"* (One is not a man in order to be a Christian, but rather one is a Christian in order to be a man).

7

Making Peace in the Nuclear Age

by JAMES DOUGLASS

POPE JOHN died fearing a global war. "I am afraid, I am afraid," the Pope said on his deathbed, "I fear that my children might become involved in a new war." After a requiem mass for John, Monsignor Loris Capovilla, his private secretary, quoted these words among his last. He recalled that the Pope had been in the Italian Army medical corps during the First World War and carried from that experience a permanent "horror of massacres and tortures of so many young lives." "That one avoid war was the thought that assailed the dying Pontiff."

The agony of nuclear war was also among the first thoughts of John's pontificate. In his first encyclical, *Ad Petri Cathedram*, he emphasized the "utter blindness" of men "rapidly slipping into a new and terrifying flare-up of war." "We repeat 'utter blindness'; for if, and may God spare us this, a new war breaks out, the potential destructive power of the arms that have burdened our age promises and holds out to all, the victor as well as the vanquished, nothing other than immeasurable destruction and complete ruin."

The only time Pope John ever mentioned modern war and justice together in a papal pronouncement, it was to reject any possibility of their agreement: "It is hardly possible to imagine that in the atomic era war could be used as an instrument of justice" (*Pacem in Terris*).

But the words of peace were on his lips constantly. John expressed peace in his every action as if trying to teach the world a way of divine life it had to learn in order to maintain human life.

If an unceasing drive for peace and a horror of a nuclear cataclysm constitute a major part of Pope John's legacy, Schema 13 is the place for the Johannine Council and the people of God to explore it in earnest. Pope John's work and suffering for world peace were closely linked with his efforts through the Council to steer the Church toward reform. Together they formed a single response to men's profound need for a Church radiating Christ in the heights and depths of the modern world. It is in the perspective of a lifelong testimony for peace unequalled since the time of St. Francis that one must therefore set the work of the Council Fathers on peace and nuclear war. Given this testimony and the authority of its final words, all men of good will can hope that John's deathbed fear will serve as a prelude to a powerful response by the Church in Council to the threat of the world's "immeasurable destruction and complete ruin."

The Council Fathers spent about an hour in all, during the mornings of November 9 and 10, 1964, discussing the moral problem of nuclear war. One speaker pointed out that the issue before them was capable of swallowing up the Council's pastoral achievements together with most of the human race, but he received little response in either the *aula* or the press.

From the assembly of more than 2,000 Fathers, 18 had asked to speak on war and peace in the debate on Schema 13's section 25, "On Making Lasting Peace." Eight, presumably representative of the range of opinions, were granted the opportunity, and one of them used it to extol brotherly love without referring to the specific issue of war.

English Mill Hill Father Arthur McCormack has noted that after the First Vatican Council, which ignored the industrial revolution and its social consequences, the workers could hardly lift their eyes from their misery to rejoice in the definition of papal infallibility. A similar point could be raised in regard to Vatican II and nuclear war: whether the Church in Council, by spending an hour of debate on the threat of man's global self-destruction, has shown a deep enough concern for the world to be worthy even today of the dialogue she so much desires with it.

The principal and virtually only point of contention among the Fathers was over how comprehensive the schema's condemnation of nuclear weapons should be. The draft of the schema condemned such weapons in the following terms: "the use of arms, especially nuclear weapons, whose effects are greater than can be calculated, and hence cannot rationally be controlled by men, exceeds all just proportion and therefore must be judged before God and men as most wicked."

Bernard Cardinal Alfrink, Archbishop of Utrecht, Holland, the first of the seven speakers to treat the question, was in favor of strengthening this statement to a clear and absolute condemnation of any and all nuclear weapons so that a so-called "clean bomb" could not be said to lie outside it. Melchite-rite Patriarch (now Cardinal) Maximos IV Saigh and Bishop Jacques Guilhem of Laval, France, also called for an absolute condemnation, and following a recurring thought of Popes John and Paul both appealed for a redirection of the billions being spent for armaments to the aid of that two-thirds of the world suffering from hunger and poverty. Bishop Franz Hengsbach of Essen, Germany, asked simply that the schema go beyond Pius XII's and John's pronouncements, and Bishop Alfred Ancel of Lyons, France, was concerned with pointing out an apparent contradiction in the text. The two remaining Fathers, Archbishop George Beck of Liverpool, England, and Bishop Philip M. Hannan, Auxiliary Bishop of Washington, D.C., believed that nuclear weapons could be used to wage a just war according to theological principles and drew on certain military data to support their arguments.

Taken as a whole, the primary characteristics of the discussion were brevity and omission. Some of the problem's aspects which the speakers failed to touch on were the right to conscientious objection, Catholics' past participation in enormous war crimes by an unquestioning submission to authority, the Church's role in a deeply divided world, a theology of peace, and the relevance, if any, of the life and teaching of Christ to the possibility of reducing man and creation to a smoldering dump of ashes.

The support of a majority of the speakers for a stronger statement against nuclear weapons provoked a question as to the Council's competence for such a statement. Council *peritus* Monsignor George G. Higgins at the American Bishops' Press Panel insisted that the Council lacked the technical competence to make any judgment on nuclear weapons, and that an attempt to solve some extremely complex problems in a few words would be "demagogic." In taking a similar position, Bishop Hannan's intervention corresponded at several points to the views of six Americans belonging to the State Department, Defense Department, and Catholic Association for International Peace, who had submitted a critique on the schema to the commission responsible for it, advising among other things that the effects of nuclear weapons are certainly not greater than can be calculated, so that in their opinion the schema's condemnation was meaningless.

This objection had the one value of calling attention to the schema's use of the terms "incalculable" and "uncontrollable," which seemed to suggest a technical judgment and thus invited such rebuttals by weapons analysts and a technical debate that could only end by deadening the document's moral impact. The terms themselves were unnecessary to the prohibition and failed to make clear that the kind of "control" at stake in the issue was specifically moral: not a measurement of the physical effects of a weapon which might in fact have obliterated a city, but rather the traditionally taught duty in justice to distinguish a military from a civilian target, combatants from noncombatants, soldiers from civilians. The text stood in need of revision, therefore, to show clearly that its key notion was not the technical category, "nuclear," nor the technically suggestive "incalculable and uncontrollable weapons," but instead the underlying, morally definable category of indiscriminate killing by weapons of total war, whether they be nuclear or "conventional." Chemical and bacteriological methods used for such a purpose would be equally immoral.

At the same time the appeal by several Fathers for a universal condemnation of nuclear weapons as such reflected their prudent recognition of the near-identity in the practical order of such weapons with total war. Their approach had the value of recalling the fact that the schema was, after all, not being addressed to moral theologians and weapons technicians, nor even only Christians, but to "all of God's children." Besides being morally precise, the schema had to be concrete enough to be rhetorically effective—its purpose was to speak to the world.

Unfortunately, none of the speakers showed enough awareness of both of these requirements, moral precision and rhetorical effectiveness, to propose an amendment that would satisfy each. This could have been done by a condemnation of the methods of total war (the use of massive weapons which strike indiscriminately at combatants and noncombatants) but specifying nuclear weapons as chief among them, thus showing the statement's practical relevance but qualifying the practical term by a distinctly moral category. The question of technical competence would then be beside the point, since the basis for judgment would be a practical moral distinction applicable to every weapon of war, and the object of judgment, total war, a moral category cutting across all nuclear and conventional boundaries. The specification of nuclear weapons would indicate the statement's primary application but would remain subject to the ruling moral category. The use of any nuclear weapons, "clean" or not, "strategic" or "tactical," would fall under the prohibition unless its use could be shown to be of a different moral character. In short, the burden of moral proof would rest on those who fire the missiles, not on those at the point of impact.

But although none of the speakers combined the elements of a precise, meaningful declaration, the support of the majority for a stronger statement, whatever its form, reflected their concern for the rights to life and home of the innocent in the face of a massive threat to both. While it must be admitted that the Church's moral tradition on war has certain grave inadequacies, particularly in the area of authority and personal responsibility, the inviolability of the innocent has been the one hard and inerodible diamond of the Christian tradition, as one Catholic writer has put it. This moral protection of innocent life has been an integral part of the Church's teaching wherever the right to life has been threatened, from abortion to obliteration bombing. What Pius XII said in 1951 can be affirmed as a fundamental tenet of Catholic teaching:

"There is no man, no human authority, no science, no medical, eugenic, social, economic, or moral 'indication' which can show or give a valid juridical title for a *direct* deliberate disposing of an innocent human life—which is to say, a disposition that aims at its destruction either as an end in itself or as the means of attaining another end that is, perhaps, in no way unlawful in itself. . . . The life of an innocent person cannot be touched."

It is for this reason, the Church's traditional defense of innocent life combined with the unprecedented threat to life everywhere from nuclear weapons, that Bishop Hannan's and

Archbishop Beck's interventions struck many as being preoccupied with the wrong problems. Bishop Hannan's objection to any conciliar declaration against nuclear weapons—"that there now exist nuclear weapons which have a very precise limit of destruction"—is true enough but of questionable relevance. It ignores the fact that each of the several thousand strategic weapons composing the backbone of nuclear deterrent forces has a destructive power towering over the Hiroshima bomb, and in many cases greater than the force of the entire Second World War. Even the relatively small tactical weapons defended by the Bishop constitute together in Western Europe, quite apart from our strategic forces, "a combined explosive strength of more than 10,000 times the force of the nuclear weapons used to end the Second World War," to use U.S. Defense Secretary Robert S. McNamara's description in 1963. It can be suggested, therefore, that the Washington Bishop's recommendation that "theologians be acquainted with the facts about modern weapons, including nuclear weapons, or be willing to secure the facts" is equally applicable to those members of the hierarchy who speak out on the question.

Archbishop Beck's intervention moved between opposite poles, reflecting the conflicting tendencies of one English school of theologians on the question of nuclear war. The intervention acknowledged in an opening paragraph that the direct killing of the innocent is "intrinsically evil," but failed to relate this principle to the later conclusion that "in certain circumstances peace can be assured only by what has been called the 'balance of terror.'" The speech also recognized the vast destructive power of most nuclear weapons, but hypothesized situations in which these might be used legitimately, as in the outer atmosphere, so that the Council should not condemn the possession and use of these weapons as essentially and necessarily evil.

This type of approach to the problem has become known as the "fleet-at-sea argument," since the usual example given of a theoretically legitimate target for the enormous weapons at hand is a fleet at sea safely removed from the world's population centers. The variation in the outer atmosphere is more contemporary, but even here a theological flight does not remove the actual threat against earthly targets, nor does it clarify the moral responsibility of men aware of the real use of such weapons.

Archbishop Beck's defense of the "balance of terror" raised the question which, even more than actual war, is central to the moral problem of nuclear weapons: a total-war deterrent. But the Archbishop's defense of the nuclear deterrent on the grounds that it has "succeeded in keeping peace however tentative" only repeated the standard political argument for the morally dubious act of threatening genocide. On the morality of deterrence the speakers were either silent or so effusive in condemning it, as in the case of Maximos IV, that the point was difficult to define. The schema itself was disapproving but evasive: "There is no true peace if wars are postponed only by a parity of weapons for spreading terror rather than by a sincere spirit of cooperation and concord." No effort was made in the schema to relate deterrence to the declaration against nuclear weapons.

In fact a total-war deterrent and total war itself constitute the same reality in two interconnected orders: deterrence in the order of intention becomes total war in the order of execution. To limit the schema's prohibition of indiscriminate methods of war, and nuclear weapons in particular, to the order of execution would therefore be to render it morally incomplete and practically less relevant.

It would be morally incomplete because from a moral standpoint a nation's public threat of the methods of total war, as manifested in their preparation for ready execution, must be rejected equally with the act of execution. The reason is that citizens called on in advance to support such a policy could only judge it on its public evidence as grossly immoral in intention—the intention to destroy in retaliation an enemy society and the millions of innocent lives which remain the heavily predominant moral category in even a modern wartime State.

By omitting deterrence the declaration would be practically less relevant because the only effective moral judgment on missile warfare is one made on the prior threat of and preparations for such war. In an actual state of war a ten-minute warning would leave one little opportunity to register a moral protest against the buttons about to be pushed. To conform better to today's technical and moral situation, the schema would therefore have to relate what it says on the use of total-war means to their threat as a deterrent.

But as important as is a declaration upholding the rights to life and home of the innocent and condemning their violation in total war and deterrence, it is neither the only nor perhaps even the most important action possible to the Council on this question. It is simply the only possibility raised by the seven Fathers who spoke. Among those who were not granted the opportunity to speak was Archbishop Thomas D. Roberts, S.J., whose intervention, submitted in writing, stressed a different dimension of the problem, the right of conscientious objection.

It is due mainly to the courageous and persevering efforts of Archbishop Roberts himself, together with the quiet work in Rome during the second session of Jean and Hildegard Goss, Catholic members of the International Fellowship of Reconciliation, that a statement on conscientious objection made its way into the *adnexa* to Schema 13. The statement recommended that the laws of the State respect those who "on account of either a witness to Christian principle or a certain reverence toward human life refuse military service in war on the grounds of conscience." In his intervention Archbishop Roberts asked that the statement be transferred from the *adnexa* to the schema in a clearer, firmer wording.

Archbishop Roberts' stress on the person's right to bear witness to his conscience introduces the dimension of action in which the Church can begin to respond to global war in a way that is more Christian than juridical. It also indicates a way out of the apparently insoluble dilemma which has become popular through efforts to harmonize nuclear strategy with traditional morality. The starting point of all such efforts has been the question: What can Western governments do when faced by the two threatening injustices of Communist aggression and their own thermonuclear means of destruction? The answers have been variations on the theme that the West can only resist one injustice by the other, that it can only deter aggression by continuing to threaten nuclear retaliation. The dilemma is therefore how to resist Communism by nuclear weapons without losing our own moral identity. The role of the Christian in this framework has been to see to it that, if the moment of truth does come, steps be taken to destroy the world and mankind as little as possible.

Archbishop Roberts' approach is centered not on Western governments but on the Christian as a person responsible to Christ. His starting point is the question: What can the Christian do when faced by these two injustices, Communism and mass destruction? The answer, not so surprising in this perspective, is that the Christian must resist both injustices, and, moreover, that he must do so primarily by drawing on those sources and ways of action which define his identity as a follower of Christ. These have their strength rooted in the Christian's conscience, which beneath political slogans, military threats, and philosophies which more often obscure than define the motives behind them, is the basic reality at stake in the East-West conflict. It is conscience, and the extent to which its power is explored, that will determine the outcome of the most fundamental struggle: between those who are peacemakers in the deepest Christian sense and those whose orientation in life impels them toward war.

A first step, therefore, on the way to a Christian response to the problem is to recover the power and dignity of the person in conscience from a system which would reduce him to an instrument in its technological process and finally to the role of pressing buttons with inconceivable effects. Archbishop Roberts' words deserve to be mounted in red letters over the control board of the Pentagon's War Room: "We have forgotten that the finger is the instrument of the human mind, the human heart, the human conscience, responsible to God for acts eternal in their consequences."

These words were intended, however, not for the Joint Chiefs of Staff but for the successors of the Apostles. In order to recall the Christian conscience to its responsibility in the face of global war, the Church herself must first acknowledge its right to an effective moral judgment. For the person's responsibility for his own actions in war and his right to conscientious objection have been neglected to the point of scandal in the recent teaching and history of the Church, from the submersion of the Catholic conscience in Hitler's war effort to its unquestioning role in Allied atrocities at Dresden and Hiroshima.

The text of Schema 13 did little to fill this vacuum when after condemning nuclear weapons it gave no counsel to the Christian ordered to use such arms. The *adnexa's* statement on conscientious objection, besides being relegated to an appendix, received less weight still by the emphatic reaffirmation in the same paragraph of the most abused rule in just-war casuistry: the presumption of right in war to government authorities. In view of the stress given this rule in the past and the consequent moral tragedies in the context of modern nationalism, its right to a place anywhere in the schema or *adnexa* should have been questioned severely, particularly in conjunction with the Church's long overdue recognition of conscientious objection.

To restore to the Christian conscience its power to resist

and counterbalance the enormous energy being expended on genocidal weapons, the Council could reinforce an affirmation of the right of conscientious objection in the schema proper by directing Christians toward a rediscovery of the Scriptural roots for a personal witness to peace. These are not hard to find—they constitute an essential part of the Gospels—but their relevance to war, and to modern war in particular, has been obscured by a scholastic ethic whose interpretation of the Gospels has involved a systematic de-emphasis of Christ's nonviolent teaching. The meaning of these Gospel texts has been obvious enough to men like Gandhi to provoke wonder at Christians who would fit them into a just-war ethic. In view of both the Church's deepening understanding of Scripture and of nations' profound involvements in the machinery of total war, there would be nothing imprudent in the Council's support of a Christian dedication to total peace, especially by a recommendation in the schema that each Christian explore in conscience the nonviolent love and teaching of Christ. The subsequent impact of the Prince of Peace on the course of history might well be greater than it has been through the just-war doctrine.

To the objection that such an approach could lessen Christian participation in certain sectors of the political order, the answer is that the scholastic ethic itself bears with it a hard recognition, untempered by any priorities in a fight against an external enemy: that to the extent—and no further—that nations are committed to murderous means of defense, the political order has become divorced from the moral order, and Caesar from the Christian's allegiance to God and man. The split between these two normally converging orders is a wound extending to the heart of the body politic and into the conscience of each citizen aware of the price set today on national security. It is a wound that will only go deeper through those efforts which in fact sacrifice the moral order to the political. The Christian ministers to this wound through the service of reconciliation: resisting injustice wherever he encounters it, making peace in the world as one in-formed by the life and teaching of Christ, and widening that community of love and reconciliation which is the Church in her fidelity to God. If this service must sometimes be performed elsewhere than at the center of the political order, its ultimate effect on that order is no less for its obedience to the Lord of History.

Any political effort by Christians, especially their spiritual leaders, to balance moral imperatives by national allegiances when the existence of the human race is threatened carries grave dangers for both the Church and the world. It is clear now, whatever one's final judgment on *The Deputy*, that the Church cannot remain prudently silent before genocide and still bear an effective witness to Christ. When confronted by a massive threat to God's children, love demands that the Church speak out. It is of the very nature of love to express itself, sometimes to cry out in protest when it is a question of the image of God being violated across the world. To remain silent in such circumstances, however apparently weighty the reasons of prudence, is inevitably to suppress an essential element of love and thus of Christ. Although silence can often bear a positive meaning, in the case of the Church faced by mass murder or its prospect the only sense that a watching world will ever see in prolonged silence is simple withdrawal.

The "thermonuclear umbrella," to the extent that it is identified with "Christian nations," is for the Church no political protection against atheism but rather an intolerable shield between herself and the world she was meant to serve in Christ. Split visions of the world are common to a technological age when basically inhuman occupations can be pursued with a minimum of awareness, but there are few visions so split as that of Christians professing the Gospel of universal love while simultaneously supporting the threat of global destruction. When we speak in particular of the benefits of a balance of terror, we should be careful to distinguish a good way of life from a deeper way of faith which, however, to the non-Christian world is apparently upholding and upheld by thermonuclear terror. This is not the problem of a bad image, of the difficulties involved in selling a politically realistic brand of Christianity to those having a less sophisticated (and perhaps more Christian) moral vision, but rather a question of making one's faith and love incarnate in the world.

Is it really so naive for men to ask, if Christ died out of love to save the world, what right have his followers to join in its destruction? Or does the question indicate a deeper sense of the Gospels than can be found in a Catholic answer based on facile distinctions between body and soul, this life and eternal values, existence and a transcendent purpose, all of which distinctions, however valid in themselves, if seized on in isolation and pushed blindly to their otherworldly limits could harden us to the prospect of inconceivable crimes in this world? Such a religiously dressed approach to nuclear war, with its flat rejection of a world in crisis for the sake of eternal values, would only confirm the Marxists' charge of a Christianity indifferent to man and match their own indiscriminate choice of means to an end. If the Church is to manifest to the world the love of its Creator, she cannot condone through silence a wholesale disdain for man and creation through the threat of total nuclear war. When the rights of the innocent and human life itself become so neglected as to allow casualty estimates for another war to range upward through the hundreds of millions, divine love demands speech in the strongest terms possible, even at the risk of political oblivion for the Church and her members.

But in fact a conciliar condemnation of total war and support of a Christocentric nonviolence would very likely have favorable political effects for both the world and the Church, and despite conflicts with national policies, would in the long run strengthen the Church's moral influence in the international order. Those who fear that a declaration against nuclear deterrence would reduce the Church to the role of an ineffective sect in relation to mankind have little sense of the way in which moral power today becomes politically effective.

It can be said, for example, against one overly pragmatic Catholic approach that it is not by infiltrating the ranks of Western defense departments that Catholics can make their strongest contribution toward world peace. This is not because defense departments are inherently evil, but because weapons developments and policies in the nuclear age have gone so far beyond moral limits as to make military strategy surely one of the least promising areas for peacemaking. The mistake in this approach is to identify effective moral power with the most immediate responsibility over the instruments of annihilation. The opposite may be closer to the truth: that a certain distance is here an imperative for any significant moral influence.

The power of the papacy to make peace in the modern world has never been more evident than under the hand of Pope John, whose distance from any approval of nuclear policies was astronomical. Despite the world's increasing attention to John in his last days and its reverence for his memory, we are still far from an appreciation of the profound role he played in the East-West drama from the beginning of the Cuban missile crisis to the preliminaries of the test-ban treaty. Now that the three principal figures in that drama, Kennedy, Khrushchev and Pope John, are either dead or in obscurity, it can be hoped that relationships which one could only sense before will be documented fully.[1] But even lacking the inner dimension of the story, we know the immediate moral impact on the international scene of *Pacem in Terris*, which even at the time of this writing, almost two years after the encyclical's

[1] A first step in that direction is an article by Norman Cousins in the *Saturday Review* (November 7, 1964) on his negotiations with former Soviet Premier Nikita Khrushchev on behalf of the Vatican for the release of Ukrainian-rite Archbishop Josyf Slipyi of Lvov, USSR, and Archbishop Josef Beran of Prague. (Both prelates are now cardinals.)

publication, was the subject of an international convocation addressed by the Vice President of the United States.[2]

[In the case of John, a moral voice was heard and became relevant, not by issuing politically cautious suggestions, but by remaining absolutely faithful to its own standards of truth: "the fundamental principle on which our present peace depends must be replaced by another, which declares that the true and solid peace of nations consists not in equality of arms but in mutual trust alone (*Pacem in Terris*)."] There are significant differences between Pope John in *Pacem in Terris* and the Vatican Council in "The Church in the Modern World" but none so great as to indicate that a strong conciliar declaration against nuclear policies and for a nonviolent Christian position, with its Johannine background, would provoke the kind of reaction that would force the Church to retire to a ghetto. On the contrary, the statement would likely have the value of reducing East-West tensions in the same way that *Pacem in Terris* did—by presenting imperatives which however much in conflict with current policies are immediately applauded by national leaders for their underlying vision and urgency, thus bringing the vision into political focus and that much closer to realization. Such a statement would have the further effect of redirecting the work of a large number of Catholics away from nuclear arms and policies and toward those institutions, found in both national and international politics, which serve directly the cause of world peace. The subsequent pressures on governments to help strengthen these

[2] Pacem in Terris Convocation held in New York City, February 18–20, 1965, by The Center for the Study of Democratic Institutions. Program participants included Vice President of the United States Hubert H. Humphrey, United Nations Secretary-General U Thant, West Berlin Mayor Willy Brandt, U. S. Senator J. William Fulbright, Chairman of the Senate Foreign Relations Committee, U. S. Ambassador to the United Nations Adlai E. Stevenson, British historian Arnold Toynbee, British economist-journalist Barbara Ward (Lady Robert Jackson) and Muhammad Zafrulla Khan, Permanent Representative of Pakistan to the United Nations.

often neglected institutions would also be a significant step toward international peace and order.

The over-all political effect of the Church's moral rejection of the deterrent would therefore not be to withdraw Catholics from public life but rather to shift them off center in terms of national political priorities, thus putting them directly on center in terms of the overriding moral imperatives for international politics. "He who loses his life shall find it," and a world-wide Church willing to risk losing a certain amount of national political influence by opposing everyone's nuclear deterrent might well find herself, like the neutral powers in the United Nations, with an increasing moral prestige and a deeper, wider influence in the work for world peace. It is this kind of independent peacemaking role which Pope Paul seems to have had in mind for himself when he wrote in *Ecclesiam Suam:* "We shall be ready to intervene, where an opportunity presents itself, in order to assist the contending parties to find honorable and fraternal solutions for their disputes." Paul conceives of this peacemaking function as "a loving service to the world." The Church's vocation in the midst of conflict remains always one of reconciliation, as the universal mother of warring sons.

Unlike any neutral nation, however, the Church is herself an international body, not founded on a constitution but united in Christ, so that her conciliar commitment against nuclear weapons would generate a moral force throughout the world, spiritual in nature and seeking political expression wherever possible. The individual Christian embracing this commitment would have to apply it in conscience to his own political situation. While unilateral disarmament is the logical political conclusion of such a position in the abstract, it is hardly one that could be realized immediately by a few Christians and peacemakers against the determined opposition of a mass of fellow citizens. The practical wisdom of a campaign for unilateral disarmament can also be questioned. It is worth recalling here Pope John's words in *Pacem in Terris* to those "enkindled with the desire to change the state of things, as if they wished to have recourse to something like a revolution": "It must be borne in mind that to proceed gradually is the law of life in all its expressions; therefore in human institutions, too, it is not possible to renovate for the better except by working from within them, gradually."

A Christian effort to transpose its moral commitment into the political order could not compromise itself by supporting the deterrent in any way as a temporary expedient, but it could nevertheless work through existing institutions and without demanding that an entire body politic be converted overnight to a difficult moral vision. The problem with recommending unilateral disarmament now for the nuclear powers is that for the policy to be politically feasible it would require first a moral conversion of almost miraculous size and depth which would itself involve gradual political steps short of such disarmament. Such an awakening of conscience might just as easily take the direction of the national sacrifices necessary for a preferable multilateral agreement and effective world government. In any event, none of these morally desirable ends is now in sight, and to recommend and work for their prior steps—necessary in terms of one's growth in community—is therefore the political expression in means of a moral commitment to the end. In the meantime, the nuclear deterrent will remain as objectively evil as before, but rejected by a widening community of citizens seeking the means for its removal. In short, the Council-inspired Christian striving for a disarmed international community would have to begin by acquainting himself and his neighbors with the political as well as the spiritual means for reconciling peoples.

It is a vision of the Church preparing to work across the world as a community of reconciliation which the Council in Schema 13 must manifest to peoples committed to destroying themselves and mankind, if necessary, for the sake of national sovereignty. The Church's power of reconciliation, like that of each Christian, is derived from Him who by the blood of

His cross reconciled all men to God. It is therefore a power universal in its thrust, if not always in the expression given it by Christians. But as the Church through her members learns more and more to open herself in every way to the entire world made through Christ, she can only widen her commitment to peace beyond all barriers in an indiscriminate witness of love.

In thus widening her commitment to peace, the Church will also strengthen the kind of power proper to her in international politics: that of a world-wide community of love exploring the possibilities of reconciliation, but resisting every act of injustice. The other side of the Church's love for all peoples must be her "program of condemning injustice wherever it appears," as Pope Benedict XV described his policy in the First World War. Her twofold work for peace, the ministry of reconciliation and a resistance to all injustice, is in principle one, for it is men's basic rights, whether it be the right to live in peace in a free society or the primary right to life, which the Church seeks always to protect in her devotion to peace on earth. Her purpose in her relations with the massive powers of modern states continues to be directed beyond all governments to the person, and, wherever necessary, to a defense of his dignity and rights as a son of God. Interpolating Pope Pius XII's statement, we can affirm as a foundation of all Catholic work for peace the truth that: "The life [and other rights] of an innocent person cannot be touched."

The Church as a community of love and reconciliation is also the basis of the theological response to the deepest question raised by a world in danger of destroying itself. The question is: If history is moving toward an absurd act of global suicide, what meaning can be found in mankind's struggle and growth upward in time? From the standpoint of reason, such an end would seem a revelation of the absurdity of the entire historical process and of the creature at its center. The imminent nature of this question and the failure of men to find an answer has contributed to the mood of despair which drifts through modern cultures. A threatened mankind's search for its own meaning may also be a reason why so much hope has been inspired by the prospect of the Council's schema on the Church in the modern world. [One thing is certain: that the Council cannot hope to reply to such a question by restating the just-war doctrine.] The spiritual crisis raised by nuclear weapons is centered not on the problem of waging war justly but on the preservation and meaning of man in history.

Christians have sometimes avoided this deeper issue by claiming that the doctrine of the second coming of Christ has ruled out the possibility of the world's ending through a nuclear cataclysm. It is true that from a Christian standpoint the end of history will occur through divine intervention. But as Josef Pieper has pointed out in *The End of Time*, according to the apocalyptic prophecy history will reach both an intrahistorical and an extrahistorical end, distinguished from each other by the act of transposition of the temporal world into the untemporal mode of the Creator. Moreover, the historical process will evoke this divine transposition by arriving at an end-situation in time which will be utterly catastrophic in character. It is this end-situation which man will create in history and for which he must bear the responsibility. Regardless of the precise nature of the catastrophic end-situation, veiled from us by apocalyptic symbolism, Christian prophecy gives no support to the assumption that the *parousia* has made impossible a final global crime by man. In fact taken by itself the prophetic teaching tends to suggest that very possibility.

The truth is that we have no theological grounds for believing that human freedom, with its profound possibilities for both good and evil, will be any more restricted in its use of thermonuclear weapons than it has been with the instruments which men of our time employed at such places as Auschwitz, Buchenwald, Dresden, Hiroshima, and Nagasaki. These events constitute a modern revelation of one side of man. Through them believers in a providential God have had to confront the terrifying latitude given human beings in history for the exercise of their own freedom. We have been forced to recognize that in terms of human freedom there are simply no limits to the evil man can inflict on man.

The Christian cannot rule out the possibility of global suicide any more than he can harden himself to it by withdrawing into a realm of eternal values. The question asked by the world is a real one: What meaning can we find in a creature whose life and progress seem stricken in time by a crisis that will end in his self-destruction?

The Church as a community of divine love meets this question in terms of the mystery of the Cross. The world confronting the possibility of an "eschatological war," the possibility of its own termination in an absurd act of human violence, can be compared to a philosopher faced by the reality of the dying Christ. To a man of reason standing beneath the Cross and watching life depart from the man, Jesus, what kind of meaning could be assigned to that murderous event? And if the philosopher had access to a partial revelation, the single truth that this dying man was the Creator of the cosmos, what good for the human race could he possibly see in the God-man's murder at the hands of His own creature? Yet to the Christian with faith in a fuller revelation an act of such apparent absurdity and cosmic evil is seen as the supreme good of creation. To him the process of man's Redemption is understood as a way of suffering and victory through apparent defeat. According to the vision of the man beneath it, the Cross is either futile, absurd, or redemptive. But even when seen by the believer as redemptive, the Cross is still understood only as mystery, with a meaning reached through faith and deepened through personal love and sacrifice.

Can we conceive of an analogous mystery unfolding at the end of that history over which the murdered God-man reigns? What meaning might Christian faith sense in the threat of global destruction? It would be a meaning dependent on the continuing presence of Christ and His Cross in history. To sense any meaning at all beneath so enormous an evil we would have to presume that the Cross had become the effective symbol and pattern of Christian action in time. The Church as Christ's community of love would have had to embrace His redemptive mystery in its darkness, accepting the truth in her daily life that her most authentic realization in history must often take place under the guise of futile sacrifice.

To the extent that a suffering love for God and man can be realized in time, and a supreme witness given to the sacredness of a creation destined to become a New Earth, the process of Redemption will continue in and through history's final crises —even if these should involve man's desecration of the entire world. In that case, the meaning of love fulfilled in sacrifice can be conceived in the final form of a communal life in Christ dedicated to the waging of total peace on earth and achieving victory through apparent failure: the Church in community embracing the world in division and agony and evoking the Return that Christians await in joy.

But to begin meeting the world today with the kiss of peace and the service of reconciliation is the most effective way for the Church in Council and all Christians in practice to prevent so extreme a crisis. Speculations on the meaning of a possible nuclear cataclysm are of value only insofar as they prompt present action. Whether or not we ourselves are entering the agony of an "end-situation," the mandate of Christian love for our age of total war is clear enough to inspire the Church to a work for total peace.

8

A Protestant Surveys
a Common Bond

by CLAUD NELSON

THERE was a time when it seemed that a great many odds and ends were being relegated to Schema 17, and one wondered whether the Council would ever get around to their consideration, and whether if it did it could make anything of them but an uncoordinated jumble, not particularly relevant or vital. When, as Schema 13, "The Church in the Modern World" was brought to the *aula*, there were still cries of "platitudes," "a rag-bag," and the like. But as it has been examined, defended, explained—and pondered—it begins to stand forth as an imperative and in some ways the crowning part of the Council's work. Certainly the Protestant delegated observers are taking it seriously; several of them have shared with me their reflections.

De Ecclesia, taking full advantage of the doctrine of development, has declared what the Church considers herself to be.

Schema 13 begins to spell out for today's troubled world what the Church is for, in human and terrestrial terms. The acknowledgment of its obligation to do this, and the invitation to the world not only to listen but to enter into dialogue, may well prove to be more important, more productive, than the solutions that the Council is ready to offer. These may be tentative or incomplete in some cases, but they are guidelines to continuing discussions.

To undertake such a statement is to challenge every worshiper to be mindful not only of self and of heaven but mindful, also, of his divine call to act as a citizen of the coming reign of Christ on earth. Schema 13 is intimately related to the constitution on the Liturgy also because its aspirations for peace and good will desperately need the support of prayer. Sincere prayer binds one to action. A Protestant hymn of my childhood, perhaps inferior in the judgment of the hymnologist, looked for progress "when all Christians shall vote as they pray"—still a timely aspiration.

"The Church in the Modern World" will be largely conditioned by the practical working of *collegiality*, not only, or perhaps chiefly, by the representative voice of the bishops expressed in Rome, but also by the action of episcopal conferences to implement Schema 13, and to carry on the dialogue in the particular "world" of their respective areas, and by the active and effective assumption of a global responsibility by the bishop of every diocese—and, within due and necessary limits, of every priest and all Religious. Without Schema 13, the exaltation and exhortation of the laity in other Council statements might remain as, in large measure, pious hopes or calls to routine "service"—not insignificant, but scarcely world-shaking. This statement, however, may well become the charter and the summons to a continuing crusade of lay men and women—the vast majority of the "people of God." This summons and charter may be susceptible of a more specific and impressive formulation than in the present text.

Considered in the light of the decree on Ecumenism,

Schema 13 is implicitly a call to all Christians. There are points at which the invitation might be made more explicit in the text. That such invitations will be taken seriously, and with fraternal appreciation, was not to be doubted, but is aptly and emphatically evidenced by action of the World Council of Churches, Enugu, January 1965, in arranging to set up, with the Vatican, a group to provide for continuing discussion, much of which will have to do with subjects considered in Schema 13. The spirit and approach of this document, and specific suggestions for cooperation could encourage such undertakings in various fields, as at the 1963 Chicago National Conference on Race Relations, with direct social benefits and no less important ecumenical by-products.

Significant comments on the relevance of Schema 13 come from two Europeans. Dutch Dominican Dr. Edward Schille-beeckx is quoted in Methodist *World Outlook* (January 1965) as saying:

It is precisely in this document that the proof will out; whether the institutional Church considers itself the be-all and end-all or whether she deems herself an instrument in the hands of Christ, at the service of all mankind.

An observer, in an unpublished report to his sponsors, em-phasizes the ecumenical importance of Schema 13. As has been said above, he notes the opportunity afforded for all the Churches to find common answers and further their unity in common tasks. Going deeper, he suggests that study of the re-lation of Church and world must lead to fresh study of the nature of the Church. In this sense, he sees Schema 13 as ex-tending *De Ecclesia*.

The importance of the Council statement on relations with non-Christian religious bodies has been underscored by Pope Paul's visit to India, a visit that may well facilitate meaningful conversation and eventual cooperation with Hindus and Bud-dhists. It should not pass without notice that in many places in Asia the Young Men's Christian Association, through personal contacts with their leaders and service to their youth, has laid foundations for understanding and cooperation with non-Christian religions.

Religious tolerance and freedom are indispensable conditions for any worthwhile consequences flowing from Schema 13. Its implementation, in turn, will contribute to their spread, and to sincere acceptance of them by governments and peoples.

Similarly, whatever reforms in education, secular and religious, are proposed and effected by Vatican II will both condition and be conditioned by the dialogues stimulated by this wide-ranging schema. Think, as one example, of what education is necessary if we are even to seek world peace confidently and resolutely, and of the tremendous financial lift that would be available for education through even a 2 per cent reduction each year in military expenditures.

Not to prolong any further summoning of evidence as to the relevance, the necessity, of Vatican II's deliberations on the Church in the world, equally important reflections (for writer and reader) on economic and international portions of the schema will be presented later in the chapter.

Relevance to Pope John's Summons

The call for *aggiornamento*, bringing the Church up to date, would seem to require the preparation and initiation of some sort of dialogue with the world; this is undertaken in Schema 13. Meaningful dialogue must be contemporary in language and frames of reference. One notes with satisfaction apt mentions in both the schema and in the *aula* speeches of "the signs of the times."

Papa Roncalli's emphasis in word and deed on the necessity of a *pastoral* Council would likewise receive less than adequate response from Vatican II without a discussion of the Church in the world. As well as saving souls from hell—in part, no doubt, in order that they may be saved—men must combat the "hell" on earth around them. This is not only to protect the truth against lies, and the righteous against the wicked, but to project the truth and the "righteous" into the world; not to condemn the world, but to redeem the world through Christ who loves it. So far does the stance of the Church seem to have changed from the desperate defense of the days of Pius IX (who shall say that some such effort was not needed?) to the apostolic embrace of Pope John's charity.

Conversation with Humanists of Good Will

One may converse, enter into dialogue, with persons of good will; in the case of others there may be debate, preaching to those whose ears are not stopped, talking about the absent. Schema 13 evidences some of the necessary conditions which the Church must fulfill in order to enter into dialogue. The dignity of the human person is affirmed, with obstacles that must be overcome if such dignity is to be maintained and respected. The schema, especially in the fourth paragraph of the "Conclusion," declares the Church's readiness not only to forgive those alien to her, "but also to ask their pardon, if the defects of Christians have been a scandal to them." Humility is a wonderful contribution not only to dialogue but to understanding: without it, the conversation cannot begin with the atmosphere of open-endedness essential not only to any honest discussion but to the very search for truth. This consideration applies with especial force when the Church—as in much of Schema 13—is not engaged in proclaiming revealed truth, but in seeking practical solutions consistent with the truth she has received—solutions that depend in large measure on agreement between believers and other persons of good will. Furthermore, secular contributions of the greatest importance to human well-being are ungrudgingly recognized. On the whole, Schema 13 would seem to be adequately conceived as an invitation to dialogue with nonhostile humanists.

The question presents itself, conversely, whether the world, or that considerable and influential part of it represented by humanists of good will, is itself ready to enter into conversation with the Church. Obviously, conversations of this general sort are going on directly or indirectly. I seem to recall that a few years ago a great existentialist, Karl Jaspers, pleaded for just such dialogue. I wrote in Religious News Service from Rome in November 1964: "Meanwhile one may note a few reasons why 'the world' may be less disdainful of such a conversation than it would have been only a few years ago. First, the world is less sure of its own ability to find or carry out solutions to the problems created by nuclear power, automation, co-existence, the pressures of population on the supply of food, etc. Second, it may well be encouraged by the results of dialogue among Roman Catholics, Protestants, Anglicans, Eastern Orthodox, Old Catholics, the ancient Churches of the East, and the smaller or newer Christian Churches. And, third, the world cannot forget Pope John; it may need a continuing reassurance that his Church does not forget him."

One can be reasonably sure that when Christians are prepared for dialogue, humanists will not stand aloof.

Special Case of the Communists

It does not yet appear that Roman Catholics (or Protestants) are all of one mind as to the necessity, the possibility, the conditions of conversation at the level of Church and government at any rate, between Christians and Communists. Pope John frightened a great many people (and encouraged a great many others) by such acts as receiving Mr. Adzhubei, Premier Khrushchev's son-in-law, in 1963. In *Civiltá Cattolica* (October 19, 1963) an unsigned "contemporary chronicle" protested against Communist attempts to make the encyclical *Pacem in Terris* and that visit "the basis, or the beginning, of a 'dialogue between the Church and Marxism.'" The writer said this was "causing the naive to believe that the attitude of the Church had been radically modified." He averred that the

Communists had lumped all anti-Communists together, while in fact some anti-Communism is reactionary, fascist, easily discredited. Soon after the appearance of this article the Italian bishops issued a pastoral letter on the same subject. Much milder than it might have been before Pope John, it nevertheless made very clear that the viewpoint of the Church on Communism had not changed. The Italian press which forecast this letter a short while before it was published maintained that it was desired by Pope Paul. Pope Paul, in fact, has spoken to the same general effect in January 1965.

The Communist case and the accusation that religion is "the opium of the people" has rested, in very large measure, on evidences that the Christian Churches, particularly in Russia, were really indifferent to the welfare of the people and were urging them to subscribe to superstitious beliefs and practices. In 1935 I visited two of the antireligious museums in Leningrad. The exhibits there were completely anachronistic regarding most of Christianity then—and practically all of it now. Communist propagandists are recognizing this weakness in their case. *Kommunist*, Vienna, in its January edition, said that it would be shortsighted not to recognize the changes within the church in recent years and referred specifically to the Roman Catholic Church. It urged atheists to give up their "primitive generalizations." It advocated "close collaboration between Communists and church people in the struggle for progress and humanity," but warned that "the changing church must be considered a dangerous foe." In the opinion of *Kommunist*, Pope Paul stands in the middle between realist and reactionary members of his clergy. Schema 13 might well note the changing character of any possible dialogue with Communists and Communist regimes, and guard against our lumping all Communists together. It is, of course, possible that Vatican strategy has already developed further than the Council might think it appropriate to set forth in an official document.

Are Christians in General Ready?

All the foregoing evidence of readiness on the part of
Church authorities and unaffiliated humanists might be thought
to leave open the question whether Christians in any considerable number desire the dialogue with the world or are prepared for it. The obvious fact is that all of us, laity and clergy,
are involved in this dialogue by our acts and reactions,
whether we are consciously conversing or not. Dr. Schillebeeckx, writing on Schema 13 in Rome last autumn (document No. 142 from the Council Documentary Center), along
with some profound and some critical remarks had this to say:
"To serve a world in the process of unification; to meet the
moral obligation which a superior advancement in the West
imposes on Western man towards the whole world but more
especially in behalf of the countries in the throes of development; to draft with vision the blueprints of tomorrow de-
signed for the dynamic shaping of a temporal society worthy
of man—all that is part of what the contemporary religious
man considers as the concrete situation within which he in-
tends to live his religiousness. It is especially in the very midst
of all these tasks that he can indeed meet his religious requirements and fulfill his Christian self."

But there are conditions for dialogue beyond attitude and
desire, and three sections (16, 17, 18) in the present text of the
schema are largely devoted to them. Among them are knowledge, appreciation, charity, justice. Elsewhere in the schema
one welcomes the phrase, "the perfect justice of charity." For
of course the charity of "Lady Bountiful" is usually a poor
sop to one's conscience, or a mere exhibitionism, tending to
ignore or conceal the demands of justice. Christians are bit-
terly reproached by those devoted to justice in human relations when they preach or practice this sort of charity (I think
particularly of an eminent Jewish friend). But it is extremely
difficult to conceive or attain justice without the charity of the
Epistle to the Corinthians. The "justice" that Shakespeare at-

tributes to Shylock is scarcely to be preferred to Lady Bountiful's charity!

One is grateful for the phrase, "in the spirit of poverty" in section 17. I have long been impressed by the humility of many Catholics in ministering to the sick, the needy, the outcast, with no trace of condescension or fastidiousness. They would seem to be well conditioned for a crusade against avoidable poverty, disease, etc., which has been winning favor these past fifty years among Protestants—in America especially under the influence of Walter Rauschenbusch, Washington Gladden, and others; in Europe, adherents of *Christianisme Sociale* and similar movements. No small contribution to Catholic (and Protestant) readiness has been made by the social encyclicals of Leo XIII, Pius XI, and John XXIII. Schema 13 should leave no possibility of confusing "the spirit of poverty" with complacency in the face of avoidable, degrading poverty.

As to "dialogue," section 18 goes far to correct some unfortunate impressions based (justly or unjustly) on *Ecclesiam Suam*, and reinforced by an article in *Il Quotidiano* by as great and good an ecumenist as Father Charles Boyer, S.J. who, however, greets with warm approval the action of the World Council of Churches at Enugu, January 1965.

Why a Protestant Commentary?

The reader will have noted that little or nothing is being said in this chapter that might not be, or indeed has not been, said by ecumenically oriented Catholics. The major distinction in attitudes regarding "The Church in the Modern World" separates both Protestants and Catholics internally in much the same fashion. A large number, in each case, is excluded from the category described in the quotation from Dr. Schillebeeckx—not so much by a different experience as by a different conviction as to the Churches' responsibility. It would not be quite fair or accurate to identify supporters of Schema 13 with ecumenists, Protestant or Catholic, or Orthodox—but the extent of the identification is impressive. However, there is so much divergence as to the relation of unity to union between Roman Catholics and "separated brethren" that we ought to look further for the common bond among Christian supporters of this schema. (I say "Christian supporters" because a logical result of any theistic faith, in contrast to deism, would seem to be God's continuing attention to His creation—but the Christian bond goes beyond that.)

While Christians—almost by definition—believe in the doctrine of the Incarnation, not all think of it or constantly remember it as the expression of God's continuing and constant relation to His creation. Otherwise, the star of Bethlehem may be thought of more as a flash of light, a meteor, even a comet that will return, than as the Sun that illuminates both time and eternity, but with a heat so bearable, so inviting, that it attracts and energizes all who do not turn away from it. In such a setting as this, Dr. Schillebeeckx can say "the Incarnation teaches us that the entire human reality may ferry divine grace and can be assumed into a God-centered life." Perhaps Schema 13 represents Catholicism's final erasure of the last vestiges of the Manichaean heresy (all flesh is evil, etc.); it might be well to make it explicit and meticulous. But one should not, in the process of embracing the world, be guilty of the attractive fallacy that the Church on earth and the Kingdom of God are "perfectly identical entities." Once more, I am quoting Dr. Schillebeeckx. But I take it that he thinks that the Council and the Roman Catholic Church need the warning. It fell to my lot some fifteen years ago in Rome to type out the defense of a similar statement for a friend, a French abbé who was in effect appealing from his cardinal archbishop to the Sacred Congregation of the Holy Office. He held that Protestant, Orthodox and Catholic Churches were all erring in this sense. His earlier ecumenical advocacy had been encouraged, but this warning was not then welcome and (for no other apparent reason) he had to suspend publication after one volume of a projected series had appeared (*Dieu n'échoue pas*, published without the *imprimatur*).

Urgency

The need to make clear what audience is intended in a given exhortation or invitation, and to make clear which world, which *mundus*, is meant when the term is used in a changed context, has been sufficiently emphasized in and around the Council, and is doubtless being taken into account by the subcommissions and by the mixed commission engaged in preparing the schema for further consideration by the Council Fathers.

I should like to express a concern lest the whole tone of the schema leave the impression that there is plenty of time for the summons and the response. Fortunately, the recommendation to devote three or four years to perfecting the schema was not accepted. The situation does not require a "perfect" document, but one that will inspire action—action of course in the right direction, and based on sound doctrine.

More attention should be given, perhaps, to the relation between Christian action in contemporary society and the eschatological expectation. Unless the relation is spelled out, overemphasis on either might undercut the other. Ultimately (and always), our reliance is upon God, but I have no warrant for believing that He will justify our dependence upon Him if we do nothing to discharge the obligation that He lays upon us. I do not mean to say that the eschatological hope necessarily makes faithful believers. While the eschatology of Jehovah's Witnesses is not precisely orthodox, I found significant the documented testimony of an American Friend whom I saw in Berlin in the spring of 1940 that most of those then being executed for refusal to fight Hitler's war were Jehovah's Witnesses.

The immediacy of our summons to global solidarity is underscored by two needs: the intrinsic need to act as Christians toward those Asian and African peoples to whom the Western Churches have sent thousands of missionaries in the past century and a half, and the pragmatic need not to be less helpful than our atheistic rivals for the affection of those peoples. The desperate urgency to find measures for preventing nuclear war would need no underscoring except that some of us are benumbed by the menace, and others are putting too naive a trust in the likelihood of preserving the present apparent balance of terror. There will be, later in this chapter, further reference to the search for the measures needed.

The Schema and the Supplements

Bishop John J. Wright of Pittsburgh, a member of the mixed commission that prepared Schema 13, explained to English-speaking reporters in Rome during the Third Session that the schema's supplements (*adnexa*) could not be incorporated in the schema because the commission had not been able to devote to them the enormous amount of time necessary to evaluate them and come to the agreement required in order to recommend their adoption. But they were thought worthy to be submitted for consideration and comment, in order to facilitate the next round of the commission's work. Some of the material closely parallels certain paragraphs in the schema (both, quite appropriately, made use of recent papal encyclicals). There were several suggestions during the discussions in St. Peter's that certain material from the annexes should be incorporated in the schema. Leo Cardinal Suenens of Malines-Brussels referred to matters included in the sections on the family and on global solidarity and peace that ought to be in the schema—without specifying them. In commenting on those sections, I shall mention several of the points that he probably had in mind. The cardinal doubtless pointed them out to the commission—if he thought they could be overlooked. Surely, before this chapter reaches the reader, the commission—and before it meets, the subcommittees—will have given to the supplements enough consideration to incorporate important portions of them into Schema 13.

Religious Liberty

In section 12, "How the Church Is Related to Earthly Powers," there is mention of religious liberty. In section 20 the dignity of the human person is discussed. In the first instance liberty is related to the Church-State question. The discussion on the dignity of the human person makes possible reference to race, the legal or pragmatic servitude of labor, and totalitarianism. Should there not be at some point in the schema a more specific discussion of the relation between religious liberty and civil liberty in general? This can perhaps be done more easily and more effectively after the Council adopts its declaration on religious freedom. But the historical, logical, and ideological relationships between religious liberty as an obligation resting on the State, and the remainder of juridical liberties are close and vital and would seem to merit clear expression in the schema.

There have been both in the Second and Third Sessions calls for forthright declarations against racial discrimination, particularly by several American bishops. The very presence of African and Asian bishops presents a similar challenge. The Christian attitude against racial discrimination is implied or hinted at or briefly affirmed at various points in Schema 13, but the problem is so pressing and so universal that it would seem to require specific and coordinated consideration in a discussion of "The Church in the Modern World."

The Dignity of Matrimony and the Family (Section 21)

There is no doubt that the whole Catholic Church is taking the discussion of marriage and the family with utmost seriousness. Three prelates whose voices seem to be most effective in the Council—Leo Cardinal Suenens of Malines-Brussels, Paul

Cardinal Léger of Montreal, and Melkite-rite Patriarch Maximos IV Saigh of Antioch (now a cardinal)—addressed themselves to the subject on October 29, and on the whole went considerably further than the text of the schema. The volume and character of the discussion, inside and outside the Council, does not necessarily forecast far-reaching decisions of an official nature. For one thing, Pope Paul has appointed a special and still secret commission to investigate and report to him on one aspect of birth control. But the effect of the discussion will not necessarily be limited by the official conclusions of the Council. The three prelates' interventions had the immediate effect of opening the subject for continuing theological discussion, whereas theologians had felt inhibited before by the ordinary authentic *magisterium* of the Church. The next day, in fact, Father Charles Davis, S.J., a member of the American bishops' press panel at that time, said "my position as a theologian today is not what it was yesterday."

It is also possible, even probable, that some matters included in the supplements will be moved over into the main text. My reading of this portion reveals the following points, some of which were also mentioned on the Council floor, which would seem worthy of inclusion in the schema:

- —The equal dignity of men and women;
- —A forthright affirmation of indissolubility (marriage to be approached with this in mind);
- —The final decision in family planning (when the clergy are not ready with a clear directive from the *magisterium*) rests with the spouses, whose conscience is formed according to the Church's teaching;
- —(Underscoring the fact that the Church does not consider procreation the only purpose of matrimony—) Sterility does not invalidate conjugal love;
- —City planning should be adapted to the true necessities of families—not the contrary;

—The family, women, and adolescents should all be protected in law and in economics.

The inclusion of the third point would seem to be warranted by a more general statement in Section 14: "But if situations arise where there are no directives issued by ecclesiastical authority, the faithful must nevertheless do something; let them be bold enough on their own responsibility to take matters into their own hands according to the dictates of their own conscience, guided always by that Christian prudence that is inherent in the truth of the Gospel and the Church's moral teaching, and which always takes note of the individual circumstances in which one must act; and let conscience be aided also by all the human sciences that have a bearing on the several problems."

Professor Douglas Steere, reporting from Rome to the Friends World Committee for Consultation (October 29, 1964), referred to "un-natural" means of controlling disease and famine which have greatly magnified the population problem and observed: "The Church is beginning to find that 'natural' and 'un-natural' are no longer criteria that it can build upon in settling this question. For if the use of medicine and famine control is moral and no defiance of God's providence, can effective family control be consistently declared to be immoral?" Another observer lodged a plea with Council authorities for the *aggiornamento* of natural law. Protestantism (though not Anglicanism) has, he said, tended to a distrust of the Catholic concept of natural law, but there are Protestant ethicists now who would be interested in a reformulation of natural law in a frame of reference wider than the Roman Catholic or the Western. As one not skilled in theology I have often found difficulty in deciding what was natural and what was Roman in Catholic statements involving the natural law.

Fear was manifested in the Council that any modification now in what has become the ordinary authentic teaching of the Church would imply past error in an infallible Church. To this Cardinal Suenens replied that there was nothing "revealed" about the Church's attitude with regard to birth control and that it was subject to revision if upon searching inquiry the Church should be convinced that a revision was required. He continued: "The Council should avoid a new Galileo case. One such case in the history of the Church is quite enough!"

The need for fresh and clear thinking is underscored by conditions in two highly contrasting areas, the primitive and the superurban. An African prelate said in the *aula* that for his people it was important to emphasize the necessity of free consent and to dwell on the dignity of marriage. Four Protestant delegated observers signed a draft for a memorandum on Schema 13 containing these words: "The schema must also clearly relate birth control to the problem of overpopulation and its incipiently revolutionary power to overturn and physically outgrow all that civilization has developed thus far. The coalescence of already overgrown cities into a vast megalopolis will have incalculable effects in the dehumanizing of life in these great concentrations of population and in the erosion of human values. Man severed from his environment in nature and in understandable communities may fall below his present estate." One may reflect upon the extent of demographic change since Adam and Eve left the Garden under injunction to "multiply and replenish the earth." Parts of it seem to be replenished. Also, it is one thing to rely upon nature for the welfare—and economic advantage—of large families in a rural, agrarian economy, and quite another to trust nature when nine-tenths of the immediately visible surface of the globe is covered with artifacts of steel and concrete, as is the case for millions and millions of urban families.

The national Methodist magazine *Together* published articles by writers representing the three major faiths on "The Morality of Birth Control" (January 1965). I quote a paragraph from Bishop John Wesley Lord's article:

Our Lord was concerned about children. He would not be happy to see millions of children diseased, hungry, uneducated, uncared for, and unwanted simply because of the irresponsibility of their parents. Children should not be brought into the world unless they can receive the care to which they are entitled. It is an evil thing to perpetuate and aid methods that spawn, even as animals are spawned, millions of human beings for whom there is no adequate support.

But prudence must not degenerate into selfishness or cowardice. Bishop Lord quoted from a 1961 National Council of Churches pronouncement:

Parents need to remember that having children is a venture in faith, requiring a measure of courage and confidence in God's goodness. Too cautious a reckoning of the costs may be as great an error as failure to lift the God-given power of procreation to the level of ethical decision.

None of us, finally and especially, should forget the many ways in which our Lord sanctified marriage and the family.

(Note: Should not Schema 13 make reference to the Council statement on mixed marriages?)

On Properly Promoting Culture (Section 22)

The relation of Christianity with culture in much of the world, especially in the West, will doubtless be less affected by the somewhat general remarks on the subject in section 22 than by the dialogue, and by what the Churches advocate and bring about on poverty, race, economics, and peace—as well as by ecclesiastical renewal and ecumenical development.

There might be some amplification of the statement in the fourth paragraph that "when religion is neglected, human culture too declines and decays." By what criteria is this to be judged? Does culture accept the criteria on which religion must insist? Does religion decline when culture does? Of what religions, and of what kind of Christianity would the schema's affirmation—or its converse—be true? Interesting questions arise in relation to the Renaissance, the French Revolution, Czarist Russia, the Marxist culture, my own South, etc. Much of the interaction is imperceptible, especially when viewed from inside the given situation.

A major and pressing problem is the osmosis between a missionary religion and the culture it seeks to transform. How much of the culture of his native land can or should (or will unconsciously) the missionary import and impose along with his proclamation of the new words of life? How much of the native culture can be absorbed into Christianity—making it more readily acceptable—without distorting the faith? Obviously—at home or in new fields—religion must contribute something that transcends the culture it has to transform.

On Economic and Social Life (Section 23)

Our economic and social life must be considered by Christians with constant fidelity to the spirit of poverty and the constant aim of global solidarity (all three being related intimately to "a just and enduring peace").

This section rejects *laissez faire;* affirms that God's gifts belong to the whole human race; calls for "the just freedom of persons"; pleads that workers "in their shop life be truly and effectively recognized as associates in a common effort." Not one of these calls can be denied consistently with the aims mentioned in the preceding paragraph; not one of them but is disputed in theory and violated in practice in many parts of the world (even in the "enlightened" United States), in most cases with vigorous vocal and voting support from many Protestants and Catholics. This section cannot be considered a bunch of platitudes.

Even so, more help is needed than the schema affords. The problems, the needs, are not the same the world over. It is difficult for one pronouncement to deal with both primitive agrarian and supermechanized societies; with the borrowing and the lending economies, and so on. Neither situation is standing still, and the gap is probably widening and destined to increase unless and until Christians and humanists, capitalists and communists, leaders of advanced economies and those that have scarcely left the starting line, pool their ideas and unite their efforts. The memorandum drafted by four observers, to which reference was made above, includes these words:

Nor does the Schema take sufficiently into consideration the implications for advanced societies of automation, cybernetics and planned obsolescence in industry to keep the wheels moving. The problem of vocations in this context needs re-examination. It cannot be assumed that all jobs are vocations from God, for many of them are anti-social or, at best, socially inconsequential. Moreover, in advanced societies there is a major conflict between the Christian "duty" to consume prodigally in order to keep up employment and an asceticism and self-restraint that are troubled by overconsumption of goods and services.

A little later in this memorandum, its drafters exhort the Council (through the Secretariat):

May the Council not only state the problem of famine and poverty but also indicate ways that should be taken to check these evils. Very often the readiness of Christians to become deeply involved in these practical, technical and logistical problems of redressing the balance of global population and supply among the nations is taken as the clearest indication of our earnestness as Christians to act as brothers of the same heavenly Father. Recognizing that poverty and want of opportunity to fulfill a normal life is the breeding ground of advocates and devotees of a totalitarian communist solution to regional and national problems, the Church should be exemplary in her own stewardship of earthly goods and should also point out reliable ways in which Catholics engaged in politics on whatever level can cooperate with the non-Communist left in order to accelerate the establishment of greater social justice. The Church should reserve its call to voluntary poverty and inner asceticism to those who would not misuse or misappropriate a "sermon" on the spiritual value of poverty!

Action in the economic field, to be effective, must involve more than Catholics. In the theoretical field also there is room for consultation. For example, are the authors of *The Triple Revolution* necessarily un-Christian or immoral when they support the notion of a guaranteed income? Life in the Garden of Eden seems to have included the idea, and it does not seem to have been the chief occasion for the fall. There must be ways both of broadening the concept of "work" and of testing the readiness to work that would retain the safeguard that the capable person who *will* not work shall not eat.

As one Protestant observer has reminded the Secretariat for Promoting Christian Unity, one of the responsibilities of humans in Eden was to care for the rest of creation, as well as subdue it. He pointed to the "distressing" exploitation of nature by Westerners in many parts of Asia (what price surface coal mining in Appalachia and eroded soil in the South?), and urged the inclusion of a statement on conservation. In the "progressive" United States we are still victims of flood and fire on a vast scale. If we look at the whole world, there is room for rapid development and long-scale remuneration of a vast army of conservationists. The "fullness" of the earth is not inexhaustible.

Global Solidarity and World Peace (Sections 24, 25)

Economic advance in underdeveloped nations lowers the tension between "have" and "have-not" nations (example, fifty years of Soviet Russia), and tends also to decrease the size of families. Aid to the pre-industrial communities of a sort to encourage and facilitate their own efforts would therefore seem to be doubly rewarding. Philip Hauser, chairman of the sociology department of the University of Chicago, states in *Together* (January 1965) that present trends would more than double the earth's population by A.D. 2,000, and that only 1.5 billion of the nearly 7 billion would be in economically advanced areas. He comments: "Up to this time in history, no mass population has achieved a decreased birthrate without first achieving education and higher levels of living." Global solidarity seems to be not only a Christian virtue but a condition of survival for civilization and probably for the human race, since neither disease, famine, nor war any longer respects either natural or political boundaries. The negative solidarity of universal destruction can only be prevented by solidarity of purpose and effort for universal well-being.

The text underlines both the imperative and the immediately urgent obligation of Christians in this situation. The supplement seems to set forth more clearly that we are becoming one world through shared knowledge, communications, and actions. It also calls for education for peace.

What content is suitable and effective to prepare our present and future leaders to lead toward peace? Has the doctrine of the just war been revised—can it be—to serve as a guide in a nuclear age? Can prenuclear obliteration bombing be included in a war that Christians cannot only tolerate but inflict? The spreading of chemical or bacterial scourges? If we, especially in America, did not feel that with only a mild disturbance of conscience we could write off even desperately crippling losses and still emerge as "the winners," we might be inspired to make efforts for peace of the magnitude and determination that now characterize our defense measures.

Do we not need more insistence on law, and on the justiciable character of every genuine, inherent conflict of interest? It is not only such defined obstacles as the Connally measure that impede an international court: it is nationalism, and the no longer viable doctrine of unlimited and arbitrary national sovereignty. The principle of "subsidiarity"—appropriately but not too clearly invoked in the schema's appeal for mutual aid and impressively articulated in paragraphs 140 and 141 of *Pacem in Terris*—should be rigorously applied to the nation that sets itself up as the sole arbiter in an international conflict. The schema might examine the limits of coincidence between a wholesome patriotism and the nationalism that says "my country, right or wrong." Cannot Christianity say with John Wesley: "My parish is the world"? There is an embryonic movement beginning to be discussed by leaders of peace movements called "the order of humanity." Who more than the Churches should and could effectively support such a movement?

The supplement, I discovered, contains a passage for the inclusion of which pacifists have labored in each session of Vatican II. I quote Professor Steere's translation (from his report cited above): "And, moreover, in today's circumstance it appears quite appropriate that the law respect those who either because of the testimony of Christian meekness or because of a reverence for human life refuse military service in war by reason of their conscience."

Again, the question of "the just war" may intrude itself. But while the state may impose its judgment that the war is for national defense and/or the defense of freedom in the world, it should heed an injunction to respect the individual sincere conscience—religious or humanist—imposing only such penalties as tend to validate the sincerity of the objector, distinguish him from every pusillanimous or selfish draft dodger, and so prevent national confusion and demoralization. Dr. Steere reports that he found support, in private conversations with Council leaders, for the inclusion of the conscientious objectors clause. He also points out that failure to include it would diminish the significance of the expected statement on religious liberty.

Disarmament

It was President Kennedy who warned us, "either we will destroy arms, or arms will destroy us." It should be obvious by now in the light of the Kellogg-Briand and other international agreements that an agreement to disarm is not necessarily disarmament. As in other discussions of disarmament the limits imposed by national feeling and real or supposed national policy were visible also in the discussions in the Vatican Council on disarmament, and support for this point of view is to be found in some of the reports by delegated observers. The schema itself speaks of the dangers of an "uncontrolled armaments race" which seems to be slightly redundant if the hypothetical controls still permit a race. When one proposes, as some did in the *aula*, that the use in a defensive war of nuclear warheads of limited capacity be sanctioned, does he not overlook the practical certainty that once one side had employed any nuclear weapon the other side would employ a bigger one and escalation into an all-out nuclear war could scarcely be avoided? Indeed, unless nuclear knowledge were forgotten, it is difficult to imagine a war begun with bows and arrows that would not proceed to the use of hydrogen bombs. The temporary and tenuous balance of terror—always subject to unintended upsets—makes less sense with each additional nuclear power. It would approach the ultimate *reductio ad absurdum* if there were three or more top powers, each possessing an "overkill" nuclear armament. While it is probable that none of the A.B.C. weapons will be used except by accident, by madmen, or in desperation, the world has seen too many accidents, too many madmen in power, and too many nations with the psychosis of desperation to find the situation reassuring. Nevertheless, the idea of disarmament, the hope of disarmament, and every smallest step toward the limitation of arms—all are of the utmost importance, but only if they do not distract us from the real job which is to recognize that international armed conflict has become a stupid anachronism, and abolish it!

Pursuing Peace

If in fact war is stupid and men are intelligent, peace is possible. Unfortunately, millions do not believe this and other millions do not quite see how it can come about. Part of our task, therefore, is to overcome the fatalism which says that we have always had war and we always shall. Only when this is overcome will men in general focus their desires and their intelligence on establishing world peace. Maurice Cardinal Feltin of Paris has said "peace must become part of our ordinary pastoral work." This is true both because the spirit of the Gospel demands peace and can lead to peace, and also because there will be neither preachers nor congregations nor any pursuit of the other ends of the Gospel if we drift over the brink of collective suicide.

Here again the bearing of racial antagonism is important. Early in this century in connection with the Chinese Exclusion Act there was prolonged discussion and still more sloganeering devoted to "the yellow peril." It was my good fortune in 1910 to participate in a public debate in my college in which my side called for the termination of the Act, and won the decision. Without the sloganeering, the yellow peril motive, this time focused on Japan, was readily detectable among young American chauvinists when we were perfecting our national defenses in the 1930s. Let no one doubt that the cry could and would be raised again if it should seem that war between China and the United States was probable. Obviously, if the present international fragmentation and disorder continued until some combination of African states had attained a commanding position the cry would be "the black peril." Every step in the improvement of race relations which leads to mutual understanding, cooperation, and friendship is a step toward world peace.

Can the Council or the Churches all together really effect world progress toward peace? Patriarch-Cardinal Maximos IV Saigh reminds us that the bishop is traditionally "defender of the city." Speaking in the Council he urged that A.B.C. weapons should be outlawed and reminded us how much better use could be made of the money saved. In his judgment, the world is waiting for such recommendations, such leadership, from the Churches. The action of two thousand bishops not only would not go unnoticed, it would snowball, he says. Is there any cause with a more urgent or a more compelling call to the Churches to unite in purpose, in spirit, and in action?

Some General Observations

The most important fact in relation to Schema 13 may well prove to be its existence—not what it can accomplish by its recommendations, but what it has set in motion in the way of dialogue, of soul-searching, of reorientation of the Roman Catholic Church toward the world (affecting all the Churches), and, hopefully, of the world toward the Churches. The reorientation of the Churches, if developed persistently and unitedly, will be a lifting up of Jesus Christ that could draw all men unto Him.

A Protestant commentator can bring no patronizing or condescending note into his assessment of the significance of Schema 13, even though in the draft before him he sees a rather timid and temporizing beginning. But it is *only* a draft and it *is* a beginning. Protestants, after fifty years of seeking to realize how the good news of the Incarnation ought to influence society, are still too timid in their statements on peace, race, economics, mutual aid, and too divided for effective implementation of their resolutions. They can only rejoice in what is almost an about-face—at least a ninety degree turn—on the part of the largest and presumably least unwieldy of the Christian bodies.

But the situation does not call for comparisons, for compliments, certainly not for rivalry; even emulation is not too relevant. We must unite our efforts and we must lose no time. Delay in mobilizing mutual aid as required by "the perfect justice of charity" can lose our own souls and hand over most, or eventually all, of the world to atheistic materialism. Delay in creating an international system of enforceable law hastens a final judgment of atomic fire. Divided in purpose or action, we can't escape. Even united, we shall not find the right way and take the right actions in time, unless we seek and obey the guidance of the Holy Spirit.